Armin Kriechbaumer and Sue Fox

Small Dogs

Everything About History, Purchase,
Care, Nutrition, Training, and Behavior

Full-color Photographs
Illustrations by Renate Holzner

OVERVIEW OF SMALL DOGS

Small dogs were originally bred for many reasons: to be hunters, to be watchdogs, or simply to be companions. Whatever the original purposes for breeding them, they are now almost exclusively companion dogs. If chosen wisely, a small dog can be a wonderful addition to any human family.

The Role of Small Dogs

For thousands of years, people have used selective breeding to retain specific, desirable traits in dogs. People developed dogs that varied in size, shape, color, temperament, and behavioral characteristics. Because genetics affects temperament, behavior, and working ability, many breeds almost automatically do the work for which they were bred, and appear to enjoy it. Small breeds of dogs were developed for many reasons: Some were bred to go underground after foxes, badgers, rabbits, and other prey; other breeds were developed as watchdogs; some of the more exclusive breeds were created as lapdogs and companions for nobility.

Throughout the centuries, every continent in the world has produced its own breeds of small

A small dog should be part of your family.

dogs. As a result of trade and warfare, the different breeds became known throughout the world. For example, the Chihuahua originated in Mexico, the Pekingese and Shih Tzu came from China and Tibet, and many terrier types were bred in the Scottish Highlands. Even in ancient Greece, there were dogs with clipped coats and lionlike manes. Such dogs might be the ancestors of the Löwchen or the Poodle. Hairless dogs were indigenous to South America and China. The descendants of these dogs include the Chinese Crested Hairless.

Whatever their original function, small dogs are now kept almost exclusively for the companionship they provide. Pet owners consider dogs part of their family. In the past, a dog that did not perform "work" was scorned as useless. However, modern society recognizes that dogs provide benefits as pets, and certainly, the role of many small breeds as watchdogs is still highly valued.

Just like some big dogs, this Yorkshire terrier enjoys swimming.

Small dogs differ from large ones only in terms of size. Apart from that, small dogs are emphatically regular dogs, but they do have advantages over large ones. They can live happily in a city apartment while a large dog might be miserable in one. Small dogs require less exercise and eat less food. When trained, they are capable of the same good manners as their larger relatives. On average, the life span of small breeds is greater than large-breed dogs.

Problems of Small Dogs

Small dogs come with their own set of problems, not the least of which is the real possibility of being accidentally stepped on or being hurt by a closing door. Some are delicate and can break bones when enthusiastically jumping on and off furniture. Because of their size, many small dogs are overly subject to the trend to make them into little children. They are pampered with fashion clothes and luxurious dog beds and often prevented from being "real dogs."

Small Dogs and Owners

Small dogs and their owners can form intensely close bonds. Pet owners are more likely to share furniture, including their bed, with a small-breed dog than with one that is larger. Being able to snuggle a dog in your lap and easily carry him about leads to a close relationship. Unfortunately, this closeness can also lead to problems unique to small dogs, including the stereotypical picture of the snapping and yapping dog held in the crook of an arm. The information in this book can help you raise a well-socialized small dog that is less likely to engage in such behaviors.

Some small dogs won't mind being dressed up for special occasions, but always remember they are still dogs, not little people.

When you purchase a puppy, you're making a long-term commitment.

Choosing the Breed

Most people now choose a dog for the way it looks, rather than for its innate behavioral abilities. This is perfectly fine but you must also investigate the breed's innate behavior traits to make sure they are compatible with your lifestyle.

When deciding which breed is suitable consider the following:

✔ Do you have the time to brush a long-haired dog's coat? If not, can you afford to hire a professional groomer?

✔ Does your home have lots of stairs? Dogs that have very short legs and a long back, such as Miniature Dachshunds, Pugs, and Pekingese, have difficulty going up and down stairs.

✔ Active breeds need more space or more daily walks.

✔ When unsupervised, breeds such as terriers might dig in your garden. Can you provide the dog with a place in which to engage in this pleasurable (to them) activity?

✔ Do you have young children at home? Are they mature enough to know that a small dog is not a toy?

✔ Avoid buying "teacup" varieties of small breeds. These very small dogs are often not very hardy.

The elegant poodle has been a popular breed for years.

SELECTING A PUPPY

Before acquiring a puppy, there are many points to consider, such as when, where, price, and so on. Making sure that you are well prepared for the arrival of your puppy will help him adapt successfully to his new home.

When to Acquire a Puppy

Bringing home a new puppy is exciting, but it also means a commitment of time and energy. Any puppy requires your time, especially in the first few weeks when you and your puppy are establishing a routine. Plan to acquire your puppy when you will have the maximum amount of time available for his care. For many people, this is during the summer, a weekend, or a holiday (often excluding the hectic Christmas season). The least desirable times to bring home a new puppy include moving to a new home, a new job, a job promotion that might require your absence for travel or more time away from home, or when expecting a baby.

In some parts of the country, the time of year might affect your decision about when to acquire your puppy. House-training a puppy in cold, snowy weather can be difficult as both you and your puppy are likely to be miserable if the outside temperatures are freezing. Going

Glossy coats and clear eyes are signs of healthy, well-cared-for dogs.

outside can be especially unpleasant if you need to leave your warm bed to take the puppy out in the middle of the night. However, it can be even more unpleasant for your puppy whose small size makes him more vulnerable to the cold. In such cold regions, the best time to acquire a puppy might be anytime but winter.

Where to Buy Your Puppy

The best place to begin your search for the breed you desire is the Internet. Breed clubs will typically provide lists of reputable breeders in your area. For uncommon breeds, you might have to travel out of your area to obtain a puppy; many breeders will not ship small-breed puppies by air. You might also have to wait until a puppy is available.

Because small-breed dogs typically have small litters—between one and four is common—demand is often high and the prices the puppies fetch are considerable. Because of the lucrative market and their relatively small space and feeding requirements, some people breed small dogs as a cash crop. Generally, puppies from such sources are disease-prone (or already sick), and not infrequently, they develop behavioral problems. Be wary of an individual who sells several breeds of small dogs with multiple litters available at one time. Do not buy a small-breed dog from a flea market, or from someone who cannot show you the puppy's mother or who provides only vague information about the puppy's background; often, such puppies come from "puppy mills."

Breeders

Reputable Breeders

Reputable breeders are the best source for a purebred dog. Such individuals know their breed well and, when necessary, invest in genetic screening for hereditary diseases. While problems can occur in a serious breeder's stock,

they are much less likely. Such breeders are interested in and will keep track of any hereditary problems that result from specific pairings. Serious breeders who show their dogs usually have waiting lists for puppies.

Breeders of high-quality puppies will have spent time and money proving that the sire and dam are physically and mentally sound. The dogs they breed are likely to have show points or championship titles. To produce the best possible puppies, they will match pedigrees and abilities. They will raise their puppies in a warm, clean environment and socialize them so they do not have preventable temperament problems. To help with eventual house-training, many breeders provide their puppies with a separate elimination area located away from their feeding and sleeping area. By providing a separate and clean bathroom area, the breeder helps reinforce the puppies' natural tendency to soil away from their nest.

The breeder will want to know about you and how prepared you are for the puppy. Reputable breeders will usually ask you questions to make sure their puppy will fit your lifestyle. The breeder might want to know if you have small children at home and whether you will be around to care for the puppy. Breeders feel responsible for the puppies they breed and want to make sure they are placed in the best home possible. If you cannot keep your dog at any time during his life, the breeder will often take back the dog and find him a new home. A good breeder will also be available to answer any questions you might have about your puppy.

Backyard Breeders

"Backyard breeder" is a derogatory term that refers to someone who casually breeds dogs without researching the dogs' backgrounds. These are individuals who own a pet dog and breed it with someone else's pet dog without regard to health or temperament. Although some are well intentioned, other individuals can be unscrupulous and interested in money more than in the welfare of the puppies or breed. Backyard breeders are less likely to have screened the dam and sire for hereditary problems, and they might not even know that they should screen their dogs. They also might not be aware of potential hereditary problems in their puppies, which can cause you much heartbreak and unanticipated expense. Puppies from backyard breeders are typically less expensive than from a reputable breeder. Puppies that are advertised in the classified section of newspapers are typically from backyard breeders.

Some backyard breeders sell purebred puppies with no AKC registration papers. These people are likely to own dogs with AKC Limited Registration, which is a tool breeders use to protect their breed. Dogs with Limited Registration are typically pet quality and their offspring cannot be registered with the AKC. Puppies without registration papers are not usually sold for as much money as registered puppies. Purchasing a puppy from such a person is circumventing the original breeder's good judgment, and your puppy is more vulnerable to potential problems due to poor breeding.

Pet Stores

Small-breed puppies are commonly offered for sale in pet stores. Because they have not seen the puppy with his littermates, pet store

Two small dogs can be more fun than one.

TIP

Children
If you have children, choose a breeder who has socialized the puppies to the sounds and sights of children.

---

employees are unlikely to know the puppy's behavioral character. Unfortunately, you will not get the opporutunity to see the puppy's dam and cannot know about the litter's hereditary background. If you find a pet store puppy that you like, find out how long he has been in the store (hopefully not long), what kind of veterinary care he had, and be sure to obtain a copy of the pet store's health and return

guarantee. If the puppy is purebred, you should receive the registration papers.

Show or Pet Quality?

Experienced breeders will usually rate the puppies in a litter as either show or pet quality. Breeders can make only an educated guess about a puppy's show potential, based on their years of experience. When compared to their littermates that are rated pet quality, a show-quality puppy possesses certain features such as soundness of construction that more closely conforms to the breed's standard. No breeder can guarantee a puppy's show potential.

There is nothing wrong with a pet-quality puppy. He just possesses features that would make it difficult to successfully compete in conformation shows, such as coat color, but these show ring faults do not affect the puppy's ability to live a long, happy life as a pet.

Important Papers

When you buy your puppy, the breeder will give you a copy of the puppy's pedigree, a registration application, a health record, and sometimes a sales contract. Some breeders may also provide you with copies of any genetic

tests performed for your puppy's parents. The registration application transfers ownership of the puppy to you from the breeder.

Health Record

The health record includes a list of the vaccinations the puppy has received and when the vaccinations were given. It might also include a schedule for the remaining vaccinations. Whether your puppy was wormed, including when and with what, should be noted on the health record. The record will also specify whether your puppy had any other veterinary treatment. Although the health record might include a veterinarian's certificate showing the puppy is healthy, you should still have your own veterinarian examine your puppy.

Sales Contract

Some breeders provide a written sales contract that states what health and temperament guarantees they offer, while others give verbal confirmation based on their reputation. Some sales contracts contain a spaying or neutering clause, which requires you to have your puppy fixed. This is especially true for puppies with AKC Limited Registration. Reputable breeders are protective of their kennel name; they do not want pet-quality dogs that came from their kennel being bred.

Price

Small-breed dogs are relatively expensive. Depending on the breed and assuming a reputable breeder, they can sell for hundreds of dollars to more than a thousand dollars. Show-quality puppies or those from champion parents will cost even more. Do not look for a puppy on

When raised together, many small dogs get along well with cats.

sale or be stingy when it comes to price. If a seller is offering a puppy for considerably less than the breed's typical price, be wary. Expect to pay for a breeder's investment in the breed. You might think you cannot afford to buy from a good breeder, but the expense of veterinary bills from a poorly bred dog can make the initial purchase price seem insignificant.

How Old?

The best age at which to acquire your puppy is between 8 to 12 weeks of age. Many breeders prefer to keep small-breed puppies for 12 weeks to ensure that the puppies are thriving and healthy. During that time, the breeder will socialize and interact with the puppies. Never purchase a small-breed puppy less than eight

weeks old. A breeder who sells such young puppies is a novice and is trying to save money and time.

Consider an Adult Dog

Older puppies and adult dogs are available for adoption through local and national breed rescue groups. The addresses for such organizations can be found on the Internet. The reasons a small dog might need a new home include divorce, death, a family move, lack of time, abuse, and abandonment. Rescue groups typically screen dogs for health problems and temperament before placing them for adoption. If the dog's history is unknown, his reactions to men, women, children, other animals (such as dogs and cats), and everyday circumstances are

Name

Your puppy's AKC "registered name" can be long and grandiose. While the registered name is his official name, what you actually call him is referred to as his "call name" and is usually a short name.

assessed. If necessary, rescue dogs are neutered and taught basic obedience. Rescue groups know the dogs' personalities and idiosyncracies and work to make the best fit between an adopter and dog.

Once they settle into your home and way of life, rescue dogs often make loyal pets. However, you must be patient because they are not always free of problems. Rescue dogs can be more susceptible to behavioral disorders such

as separation anxiety. Adult dogs can also be more set in their ways and some might have bothersome habits such as begging or barking.

You can also contact a reputable breeder to see whether he or she knows of any available retired show dogs, or older puppies that did not fulfill their early potential as show prospects. Only consider an older puppy if he was raised in the home, not outside in a kennel.

Male or Female?

People usually have a personal preference for one gender over another, often based on previous personal experience. You should choose the gender for which you feel more of an affinity. Both sexes are affectionate and loyal and any slight differences between them do not affect these traits. Regarding trainability and obedience, there are no significant differences between the sexes. The main differences are related to size; males are usually taller and heavier than females.

Male dogs lift their leg to urinate and mark their territory. Females squat on the ground and tend to urinate all at once, rather than marking multiple locations. Intact males are more concerned with marking their territory compared to neutered males. If you have patio furniture or other items in your yard or on a balcony, you might have to teach your male not to mark those items.

Lifting the Leg

A male puppy does not begin to lift his leg to urinate until he is almost six months old,

Some small dogs need a coat during cold weather.

and some do not do so until they are a year old. Until then, the male extends his legs like a horse and goes all at once, which makes house-training much easier. Once he starts to lift his leg, you will need to occasionally supervise him when he is in the backyard so you can correct him if he urinates on patio furniture or other forbidden items.

Mounting

Both neutered and intact male dogs are more likely than females to mount other dogs for sexual satisfaction and to show dominance. The other dog will express displeasure by growling or snapping, which is usually sufficient to cause the first dog to dismount. Males might also try to "hump" a person's leg. This unacceptable behavior can be stopped by removing him and in a firm, no-nonsense tone telling him *"No!"*

The Importance of Neutering

Any differences between males and females are most apparent in dogs that are not neutered or spayed. Intact males can be more difficult to control and command. If not kept in a fenced area, they are more likely to roam. They can also become dominant and aggressive toward other males, and more likely to fight with other intact male dogs. These traits do not usually appear until the male is at least one year old. Neutering can eliminate these behavioral difficulties and neutered males generally have a longer life span than intact males.

An unspayed female will come into season (or heat) twice a year for approximately three weeks. Females in season can be messy and sometimes moody. During this time, a female is receptive to intact males and can become

CHECKLIST

A Healthy Puppy

1. Puppies should be clean and free of odor.
2. A healthy puppy will feel robust and solid and have a clean, glossy coat. He should not feel frail and bony, or have a bloated belly.
3. Long toenails and a dull coat indicate a lack of care.
4. Make sure the puppies have clean eyes and noses and that their ears have no discharge or unpleasant odor.
5. The puppies should be well socialized and confident.
6. Make sure the sales terms include your veterinarian's confirmation of the puppy's good health.

pregnant. Because she is feeling amorous, your female might try to escape to find a male. Free-roaming, unneutered dogs will congregate at your home to try and mate with the female.

Temperament

Avoid choosing a puppy from the two behavioral extremes: the shy puppy that hides or is overly submissive, and the bold puppy that shoves his way ahead of the others to visit with you. Do not feel sorry for the underdog. Puppies that are submissive can grow up to be tentative, fearful adults. They need an experienced owner who knows how to cultivate their confidence. The boldest puppy is attractive, but such an individual is likely to be the dominant one in the

Breeders' Recommendations

Allow the breeder to help you select your puppy. Experienced, conscientious breeders are interested in making the best possible match for each puppy and new owner and they are skilled at doing so. They know each puppy's character and personality. They know which puppies are aggressive and dominant, which are timid and passive, and those that are in between. Listen to the breeder's recommendation. The breeder will know which puppy is best suited to your family.

litter and the toughest to train. A bold puppy might seem attractive, but he will require more effort and time to keep occupied. Dominant puppies grow up to be adults with dominant personalities. Without an experienced owner, they can be pushy and difficult to control.

How Many?

Because of their size, it is easier for a pet owner to consider keeping more than one small dog. It is true that small dogs can enjoy each other's company tremendously, especially if you are away at work during the day. But experts differ as to the wisdom of buying more than one puppy at a time. Besides considering whether you can afford the time to walk and clean up after two dogs, and the additional expense of food and veterinary costs, there are other issues to address.

Training

Training two puppies at the same time is much more work. Difficulties arise when you must discipline one puppy without the other wincing because he thinks you are also scolding him. While training one puppy to listen to you, you can be training the other puppy to not listen to you. Two puppies will get into twice as much trouble as one, and it can be difficult to know which puppy was the mischief maker. If a mess is made in the house, you will not know which puppy needs more help with house-training.

Different Temperaments

Other more complex problems can arise with two puppies. Different dogs have different temperaments. One may respond rapidly to training, while the other requires much more work to learn the same behaviors. Two puppies will bond with each other, not with you; moreover, as they reach puberty, some pairs constantly battle for the top dog position.

You can also wait to get your puppy a playmate until he is grown, well socialized, and trained. If you get another puppy to keep your present dog company, you will need to devote just as much time house-training and teaching him as you did for your first dog. If you live in an apartment, remember that two small dogs are much noisier than one—when one dog begins to bark, the second is likely to join.

Life Span

Small dogs tend to live longer than their larger brethren. Depending on the breed, a small dog can live between 12 to 15 years; many survive into their late teens. They also

A dog-friendly adult will enjoy the companionship of another dog.

mature earlier than larger dogs. While some large- and giant-breed dogs are still filling out at 18 to 24 months, small dogs have completed all their growth by one year of age. Diet, exercise, health care, and congenital conditions are all factors that can affect a dog's life span.

Dog Parachute

Have you considered what will happen to your dog if you become disabled or meet an untimely death? Regardless of your age or health, you should make a plan for the care of your dog in case of death or disability. If you have ever perused the pet section in the newspaper want ads, you might have read ads seeking new homes for dogs whose owners have died. The well-being of a dog is often not the first thing on the mind of someone who is dealing with a difficult emotional situation.

Your beloved dog might end up at the pound or be given to a rescue group. Do not assume a family member or friend will take your dog. Instead of hoping that the person who takes care of your estate will have the time and ability to find your dog a suitable new home, be proactive. Find a willing, trustworthy family member or friend who would adopt your dog. Once you have made arrangements, be sure to keep them current since that other person's circumstances can change. Let your family know what you have arranged. Since you cannot leave money to your dog, you must make arrangements to leave it to the person who will provide your dog's care. Hopefully, you can leave enough money to cover your dog's expenses for the rest of his life. You should consult an attorney regarding how to structure the money you designate for your dog's care.

Before you bring home your puppy, you should purchase the following items: crate, exercise pen or puppy gates, bed, collar and leash, identification tag, food and water bowls, and toys.

Important Accessories

Crate

A hard plastic crate with wire ventilation is essential. Some dog owners think a crate is cruel; however, not only will a crate help you keep your sanity, but your puppy will see the crate as his own private bedroom or den and a safe place to which he can retreat. A crate is invaluable in house-training (see page 28), for trips to the veterinarian, and for car travel. Although dogs are den animals and generally do not eliminate in their dens or sleeping areas, puppies may soil at the end of the crate farthest from their sleeping area if the crate is too large. Generally, the smaller-sized crates are suitable for puppies and full-grown small-breed dogs.

When your puppy is ready for a nap, you can put him to sleep in his crate and close the door. When he is ready to wake up, he will whimper.

Creating a safe environment for your puppy is very important.

The crate will give you peace of mind and freedom to pursue other activities while your puppy is sleeping. When your puppy wakes up from a nap, he cannot void until he finds you, nor can he grab and destroy various items lying about. Fewer accidents and occasions to correct your puppy reduce stress for both of you.

Puppy Gates or Exercise Pen

Do not allow your puppy to roam throughout your entire house. A tiny puppy is difficult to see. He can unexpectedly get underfoot without you even being aware of him and this can lead to a tragic accident. Puppy or child-safe gates are necessary to keep your puppy safely confined to a single room, such as the kitchen. When your puppy has the freedom to visit you in other parts of the house, any stairs must also be safely gated to prevent your tiny puppy from accidentally tumbling down them.

A portable exercise pen is another confinement option. Expandable and portable metal enclosures are sold at pet stores. The pen will

TIP

How Not to Use a Crate

While a crate is a valuable tool, there are numerous ways to *not* use a crate.

✔ The crate is a safe refuge, not a prison or a place of punishment.

✔ Do not leave your older puppy unattended in his crate for more than a few hours.

✔ Do not lock your puppy in his crate when he is boisterous and needs to run and play.

✔ If you are away from home all day, you cannot leave your puppy in his crate.

Puppies should be supervised so they do not get into mischief.

be your puppy's secure home until he is house-trained and large enough to stay out from under your feet. While the pen can be moved from room to room, you will need to protect the floor until your puppy is house-trained.

Bed

Provide your puppy with a comfortable bed or a nest of blankets in which he can rest, sleep, and chew his toys. The bed can be in addition to his crate, or it can fit inside his crate. Either way, choose a bed with a removable cover so that it, like the blankets, can be easily washed. Puppies are playful and have no concept of how much their bed might have cost. Some puppies might decide to stalk, attack, and destroy their bed. If your puppy shows such propensities, wait to get the designer bed that coordinates with your house until your puppy is grown.

Collar and Leash

Purchase a flat buckle collar for your puppy. He might initially scratch at his collar, but he will soon get used to it. A puppy usually out-grows several collars before he has finished growing. Some economical collars are designed to expand as your puppy grows and can last for many months before a new one is needed. For proper fit, two fingers should readily fit between the collar and your puppy's neck. A collar is necessary to attach your puppy's iden-tification and leash. Buy a lightweight nylon or leather leash for walking your puppy. Do not purchase a leash with a large metal clip that is heavy or uncomfortable for your puppy.

Identification

Immediately attach some type of identifica-tion tag with your address and telephone number to your puppy's collar. Identification tags can accidentally fall off; it is prudent to write your phone number in permanent marker directly on your puppy's collar. More sophisticated methods of identification include inserting a microchip the size of a grain of rice under the dog's skin at the base of the neck. Many veterinary hospitals and shelter facilities have scanners for the microchips, which can identify the dog and the owner's relevant information. Because a microchip cannot be read by someone who finds your dog, an identification tag affixed to your dog's collar is still recommended.

Your dog should always wear an identification tag.

Food and Water Dishes

Dog dishes are available in stainless steel, heavy-duty ceramic, lightweight plastic, and hard rubber. While there are a multitude of attractive choices when it comes to dishes, the most important criteria is that the dishes are easy for you to wash. Harmful bacteria and fungi can grow in bowls if they are not regularly cleaned.

Note: Because many people do not like adding to their workload, choosing a dish that can be washed in a dishwasher makes sense.

Toys

Your puppy needs his own toys, and shopping for puppy toys is fun. An enormous variety of toys are available, but just because they are made for dogs does not mean all of them are safe. By nature, puppies teethe and destroy items, so choose your puppy's toys with care. Many older puppies are gifted at disemboweling their stuffed toys, potentially swallowing some of the stuffing and even the squeaker. Supervise your puppy's play with any toy that

he can destroy and eat. Sterilized natural bones (sold at pet stores), nylon bones, and toys made of hard, indestructible rubber are fine for your puppy to chew when he is alone.

Most puppies enjoy a few hard toys and one soft stuffed toy. As your puppy grows, you can slowly expand his toy collection. Play with your puppy and his toys but do not play tug-of-war—doing so encourages your puppy to bite harder and is also thought to encourage dominance behavior. Do not encourage your puppy to use his mouth on your hand or clothes, give him a toy instead. Practice saying *"Give"* so

Puppies need toys.

that your puppy learns to release his toy to you or other family members.

Flat rawhide chews are usually safe for puppies and dogs. When a rawhide becomes slimy and small enough for your dog to swallow, dump it and replace it. Swallowed pieces of rawhide can cause intestinal upset and blockages that might even require surgical removal. Supervise your dog when he chews to make sure he does not bite off small, soft pieces. Avoid offering your puppy or dog any hard items such as cow hooves as they can cause fractured teeth.

Pooper–Scooper

If your puppy will be confined to a backyard for his bathroom area, a pooper-scooper is indispensable. This long-handled tool can make cleaning up much easier and quicker when compared to a shovel. No dog likes to play or lounge

Your puppy might be scared and lonely his first few nights away from his mother.

in a dirty yard. Besides being smelly, droppings are prime breeding grounds for flies. Viruses and intestinal parasites are also transmitted through droppings. Furthermore, a young frolicking puppy might accidentally step in his droppings and then track them into the house.

Times are changing and more communities are enacting and enforcing poop-scoop laws. When taking your dog for a walk, a plastic bag is the easiest device to clean up after your dog. Place the bag over the dropping, pick up the dropping, and then turn the bag inside out. Your hand will always be protected by the plastic bag. Not only is cleanup required in some areas, doing so will win you the appreciation of your neighbors.

Visiting the Veterinarian

During your first scheduled visit, your veterinarian should be able to detect any serious problems that could affect him. Ideally, your puppy should be examined by your veterinarian within the first 48 hours. The veterinarian will check for conditions such as heart murmurs, infections, bite and teeth alignment, and hernias, and review a vaccination schedule. If possible, bring a fresh stool sample so your puppy can be checked for internal parasites. Your veterinarian should also discuss the symptoms and home treatment of hypoglycemia (low blood sugar) a condition that can affect small-breed puppies.

The First Few Nights

You might not sleep too soundly the first few nights your puppy is home. Expect to let him sleep inside his crate in your bedroom for the first few weeks. Keeping him next to your bed at night can help your puppy adjust to his new life. You will hear him if he wakes up whimpering and frightened, and can quietly reassure him. Persistent crying is likely to be an emergency signal indicating he needs to be taken outside to eliminate. The puppy must adjust to your life, but allowances must be made for his needs. You do not want to encourage 2:00 A.M. play sessions, so after he has voided, return him to his crate. Even if he initially fusses and complains, he will soon fall asleep. Feeding your puppy his last meal earlier in the evening might reduce the need for any midnight outings, although your puppy might also just wake up earlier in the morning.

Safety Considerations

You must puppy-proof your home. This means that potentially hazardous items, such as poisonous (to dogs) houseplants, must be removed or moved out of reach, electrical cords must be taped safely out of the way, and household cleaning products and medicines stored out of reach. Any decks or balconies should be securely screened to prevent your small puppy from falling out. As your puppy follows you about, you might see other areas that need to be altered as you teach your puppy right from wrong.

Roaming Freely

Your puppy should not be allowed to roam freely throughout the house. Instead, you should confine your puppy to one or two rooms where you can watch him. Because you want the puppy to be part of your family, the kitchen is usually best, and its tile or linoleum floors are easy to keep clean. Be sure the cupboards are securely closed. Move any poisonous products

safely out of reach in case your puppy does get into a cupboard. Use a puppy or child's gate to keep your puppy in the kitchen. Close the doors to the other rooms, and block off access to the rest of the house with inside gates.

Chewing

Puppies explore the world with their mouths and need to chew. Anything left lying on the floor, such as shoes, clothes, books, and so forth, will be tested by your puppy's mouth. These items must be picked up and put out of reach until your puppy knows not to chew them. To a puppy, children's toys can look just like his own; however, seldom are such toys sturdy enough for a puppy. Avoid the temptation to teach children to pick up their toys by letting the puppy destroy a few. If the puppy swallows pieces, they can cause digestive problems, risky surgery, and an expensive veterinary bill. Until he knows better, keep an unsupervised puppy out of the children's room and help your youngsters pick up their toys.

Outdoors

When you take your puppy outside to play in your fenced backyard, watch him for the first few times. A puppy might eat flowers, shrubs,

Small dogs enjoy attention from well-mannered children.

How to Pick Up and Hold Your Puppy

✔ To pick up your puppy, slide one hand under his chest and use the other to support his hind end. While cradled on your arm, his front legs can dangle between your fingers.

✔ Snuggle him next to your body for security.

✔ Because he is irresistible, visitors might want to also pick up your puppy. Be sure they use the proper technique. Better yet, have them visit with the puppy on the floor. Puppies can squirm and, if dropped, can be seriously hurt with broken bones or worse.

✔ When your puppy is an adult, you are likely to still routinely pick him up for snuggling. Training your puppy with a command such as *"Up"* or *"Lifting"* will let your puppy know what to expect.

and lawn furniture, and find other hazards and ways to escape that you might not know about. Some backyard plants are poisonous and if a puppy eats them, he could get sick, and even die. Lists of poisonous plants are available from many references, including books devoted to the health care of dogs, Internet sites of veterinary schools, and the ASPCA Animal Poison Control Center (see page 93), and should be reviewed to make sure toxic plants are not in your yard.

Do not allow your puppy to lick or eat any unknown substance off the ground, especially in garages or streets. The antifreeze (ethylene glycol) used in vehicles is poisonous to dogs and it does not take much of this sweet-tasting substance to kill—½ teaspoon per pound of body weight. Even with veterinary care, a dog that recovers can later die due to complications from organ damage.

Children and the Puppy

Many small dog breeders prefer not to place their puppies in homes with young children. Without constant parental supervision, the tiny puppy could be seriously hurt by a child who does not understand that the puppy is not a toy. Even well-meaning children can accidentally hurt a puppy. You must decide whether your children have the maturity necessary for a small-breed puppy or whether it might be best to wait until they are older.

Both children and puppies must learn how to behave around one another. Do not allow children to be rough or allow the puppy to nip.

Children must be taught how to behave around the puppy.

Puppies have sharp teeth that can frighten or hurt children if they play-bite. If your puppy is teething, have the children give him a toy on which to gnaw, not their hands or clothes. Children sometimes tease a puppy by wiggling their fingers in front of the puppy's face or by taking away a toy and then repeatedly tempting him with it. Children must be taught to not tease the puppy. When a dog does not want to be bothered, he will get up and leave the area. The child should respect the dog's desire and not follow him. He should also learn not to disturb him while he is sleeping. Some behaviors, such as staring down the puppy, or even kind gestures such as pats on the head, should be prohibited. Staring is perceived as a challenge and can lead to problems as the puppy matures. While larger-breed adult dogs do not resent a child's pat on the head, a small breed is happier with strokes under the chin.

City Puppies

If your puppy must use a city street for his bathroom, be sure to keep the area clean. Choose a location that is not used by other dogs to reduce the risk of infection to your puppy. House-training can be difficult for people who live on the upper floors of apartment buildings. By the time you notice that the puppy has to go out, it is useless to grab him and quickly take him downstairs to go outside—the puppy can't hold out that long.

Paper-training

In this case, you can paper-train or litter box-train your puppy. Training your puppy to eliminate in a confined area inside the house will keep your home clean.

✔ Spread newspapers or puppy training pads sold at pet stores on the floor of the puppy room.

Big city dogs require special consideration, especially if you live in a high-rise building.

✔ Place the papers away from the puppy's bed, food bowls, and water bowls to take advantage of his preference to not soil these areas. You can eventually reduce the coverage as you will find the puppy always uses one spot.

Litter Boxes

Pet stores sell litter boxes for small dogs or you can use one sold for cats. Do not expect your cat to share a litter box with your puppy. Moreover, some dogs have the disgusting habit of helping themselves to "feces snacks" in the cat's litter box. Except for the clumping variety, commercial litter is suitable for a small dog's litter box. Make sure your puppy can easily climb in and out of the litter box. If necessary, cut an easier opening.

✔ Set the puppy down on the paper or in the litter box at the first sign he has to go. Praise him when he does his business.

✔ If necessary, placing already soiled paper in his litter box or the location you selected for his indoor toilet, will encourage your puppy to go.

✔ Replace the paper or clean the litter box as soon as the puppy has finished using it.

✔ If you have a balcony (securely screened), you can train your puppy to use it as his bathroom area.

✔ When you take a paper-trained puppy outside, he might hesitate to go on bare ground. If so, bring some newspaper with you and place the puppy on the paper to encourage him to go.

Because their messes are small, some pet owners are lax with house-training. This is a mistake, especially if your dog develops diarrhea. Moreover, while young male puppies squat to urinate, they eventually will lift their leg. Indoor products, such as plastic hydrants with pans below, are available for the bathroom area of indoor-trained male dogs.

Car Travel

Start teaching your puppy when he is young how to ride in the car. Do not let him bark, run among the seats, or put his head out the window. A variety of harness restraints and even car seats are available that allow your small dog to safely and securely ride in the car. If your car is large enough, your dog can also travel in his crate.

Take your puppy on short errands to get him used to riding in the car. If you occasionally schedule a stop at a park where he can play, or let him out to visit an admirer, he will be even happier to go. To prevent a potential accident, teach your puppy not to bolt from the car. He should learn to wait until you give the command to jump in or out. Leaving a hard chew bone when your puppy is alone in the car will give him something to do while he waits for your return. If your puppy does not ride in a crate, keep your initial absences from the car brief. You do not want him chewing the car's interior. A puppy's exploratory chewing can continue for several months, during which time he might not be reliably left unattended.

TIP

Outside Temperature

Be aware of outside temperatures when you leave your dog alone in the car. The temperature inside a car can become extremely (and dangerously) hot, even when the windows are open and the car is parked in the shade. Breeds with short muzzles are exceptionally sensitive to heat. On cold or snowy days, short-haired breeds need a dog sweater to stay comfortable.

A soft-sided carrier can be used to transport your small dog.

House-training requires your time and patience. How long it will take depends on your consistency and on your puppy's ability to learn. House-training can be more difficult to accomplish if you are at work all day. The more you are around him, the greater the chance you will recognize when your puppy needs to go outside.

Small Breeds vs. Large Breeds

In general, small-breed puppies take longer to housebreak than larger breeds. Several reasons have been offered for this disparity, including

1. They need to go more frequently.

2. Their excretory systems take longer to mature.

Always bring the puppy to the same place when it is time to defecate and urinate.

3. Their genetics may be different because their lack of house manners has probably been tolerated for hundreds of years, since their messes are substantially smaller than those left by a large dog.

4. Their concept of space is different from that of a large dog, hence a small dog *does* move sufficiently away from his bed and eating area for his toilet.

Crates

A crate will make house-training your new puppy easier and more effective. By keeping your puppy in his crate when you cannot watch him, you help prevent accidents in the house. Use of a crate reduces house-training time to a minimum and avoids keeping the puppy and yourself under constant stress by continually correcting him for making mistakes.

Taking Your Puppy Outside

You will need to take your puppy outside several times a day. Puppies have four typical times they need to eliminate: when they first wake up in the morning, immediately after eating each meal, about 15 minutes after playtime, and just before bedtime.

Develop a schedule for your puppy so he is taken out at the same times each day. Along with a regular elimination schedule, feeding your puppy at consistent times will make house training easier.

Mornings

When you wake up in the morning, the first thing you need to do is take your puppy outside; carry your puppy to avoid the chance of an accident happening on the way. Give the command *"Outside"* as you leave the house. Set him down in the same place each time. Do not leave him outside by himself. You must make sure that he does his business. Stand quietly while you wait for him to go, which sometimes can take a while. Use a "bathroom" command such as *"Go pee"* and praise him when he eliminates. Then take him back inside.

If, when he is outside, he does not eliminate in a few minutes, take him back inside. Do not let him stay outside to play. This helps him learn that the outdoors is for elimination. Keep the bathroom area clean of droppings; the smell of urine will encourage your puppy to use the same spot.

Evenings

Put him in his crate each evening to reduce the chance of accidents, but be sure he has eliminated before doing so. Taking your puppy outside late at night can help him sleep through the night. If your puppy wakes up whimpering, chances are he has to go outside.

Recognizing the Need

How can you tell when your puppy needs to eliminate? When puppies need to urinate, they often stop and squat with little warning. To prevent accidents, use timing. How long was it since your puppy last went outside? If it is more than a few hours, take him outside and praise him when he voids. When puppies need to defecate, their behavior changes. They suddenly stop playing and begin to sniff around. Some might circle around and around in preparation to eliminate. Keep a watchful eye out for these behaviors. If necessary, quickly scoop up your puppy and take him outside. Be alert: your older puppy might eventually stand by the door when he needs to go outside.

Mistakes

The best way to house-train your puppy is to not give him the opportunity to make a mistake in the house. With house-training, you must think for your puppy. You need to keep track of how long it has been since your puppy last went outside. Until adolescence, many small-breed puppies cannot "hold it" for more than one or two hours after they have already eliminated. If you are vigilant, you should know before your puppy does when he needs to go; therefore, you will have few accidents to clean and there will be fewer reasons to scold your puppy.

Consider paper training or using a litter box if you live on the upper floors of an apartment.

Your puppy will make mistakes. If you catch your puppy in the act of making a mistake, use a firm *"No,"* loud enough to startle him, but do not yell at him. Do not get angry and scare him. Pick him up, take him outside to his bathroom area, and give his bathroom command. Praise him for going outside and then bring him back inside again.

If you discover a mistake your puppy already made, do not yell at him or push his nose into the mess. He will not understand why you are yelling at him and such methods can derail the house-training process and create more problems. His accident is your mistake because you did not pay enough attention. After you clean up the mess, use an odor-neutralizing product sold at pet stores to remove any scent that might attract your puppy to the same place.

Paper-training

Because house training can be challenging, many puppy owners find managing the process easier if they also use paper-training in the house, (see page 25), in conjunction with outdoor training.

FEEDING

An enormous selection of dry and canned dog foods is available today. The best choice to feed your small dog is a premium brand of dog food. Providing a nutritionally complete and balanced diet is one of the most important ways to keep your dog healthy.

The ingredients that make up premium products are typically more expensive and higher quality compared to the ingredients in grocery store and generic brands. Dogs that are fed premium foods appear healthier, with more lustrous coats, better skin condition, and fewer digestive problems. Look for premium dog foods at pet stores, veterinarian offices, and feed stores. A few brands are sold at grocery stores.

The main criterion that you should use to judge a food is your dog's response to it. After four to eight weeks of eating the food, how does your dog look? Is his fur dry or glossy? Is his skin flaky or soft and supple? Does he constantly scratch himself even if he has no fleas? Does he have a good appetite and firm stools? Does he have gas? Consider switching brands if your dog's coat does not look shiny or his skin is dry or the food appears to cause persistent gas.

Quality nutrition can help a small dog live well into his teens.

Life-stage and Specialty Diets

A dog's nutritional requirements change as he grows from a puppy into an adult, and change again as he ages. Many dog food manufacturers have developed different types of foods to meet these changing nutritional needs. These life-stage foods are labeled for puppies, adults, and senior dogs. Life-stage foods are more precisely formulated than a one-size-fits-all approach and usually incorporate the latest research findings. Feeding these types of foods can best meet your dog's nutritional needs and help keep your small dog in top health and condition throughout his life.

Your puppy's growth and development will be complete by one year of age. You can then switch him to an adult food and decrease the amount you feed him. Once your dog reaches seven years of age, consult with your veterinarian about when he should be switched to one of the senior dog diets. These foods are

TIP

Changing Food

If you change your dog's food, you should do so over a period of a week, gradually mixing the new food in with the old. While some dogs can tolerate an abrupt change, others will experience a digestive upset, such as diarrhea.

lower in protein, fat, and calories, and are designed to meet the nutritional needs of older dogs. Because older dogs slow down and are less active, their calorie intake should be decreased. Your older dog will be healthier and more energetic if he is not overweight.

Homemade Diets

Homemade foods are an alternative to commercial diets. These diets are popular with dog owners who are concerned with potential adverse effects due to the ingredients in some commercial dog foods. Preparing a homemade diet takes considerable time and effort. If you elect to prepare a homemade diet for your small dog, you should review the proposed recipes with a knowledgeable veterinarian to ensure that your dog receives proper nutrition. Some pet owners do not cook the food; they feed a homemade diet that consists of raw meats, which they think is more natural. However, uncooked meat, fish, poultry, and eggs can be contaminated with bacteria including *Salmonella* and *E. coli.* These pathogens can cause potentially fatal illnesses and for this

reason, most veterinarians do not recommend feeding raw foods.

Feeding Your Puppy

Your puppy's breeder should give you some of the food the puppy has been eating. Some breeders prefer canned food, while others feed puppy kibble softened with water. Wait at least a week if you plan on switching foods; your puppy has many other things to adjust to without a change in diet, which can cause digestive upset.

Note: Although canned food must be refrigerated between feedings, warm it to room temperature before feeding it to the puppy.

Amount

Your breeder can tell you how much food to begin feeding your puppy. Generally, your puppy will eat at least four small, equal-sized meals a day. As he gets older, you can decrease the number of meals to three, but still feed him the same amount of food. Puppies older than nine months should be fed twice a day—once in the morning and once in the evening. As your puppy grows, the amount of food you feed him should be gradually increased. Allow your puppy 10 to 15 minutes to eat each meal.

When?

Ideally, you should feed your puppy his meals at the same time every day. This will help you house-train him because puppies eliminate shortly after eating. After every meal you should take your puppy outside to do his business. Scheduled mealtimes will work only if you are home during the day. If you work during the day, the alternative method is to free-feed your puppy. Free-fed puppies have access to dry food at all times. Puppies that are free-fed rarely overeat and become fat.

Feeding an Adult

Your adult dog should have two meals a day. Small dogs are subject to low blood sugar, called hypoglycemia, which can cause weakness, collapse, and seizures. Two meals a day will help your small dog maintain a consistent energy level and reduce the risk of hypoglycemia. Moreover, mealtime is often the highlight of a dog's day; feeding him in the morning and in the evening can make the day more interesting for your dog.

Amount

Use the feeding instructions on a bag or can of dog food as a starting point for how much to feed. The feeding instructions are general recommendations, usually based on a dog's weight. Your dog might need to eat slightly more or less. The proper portion to feed him is whatever amount is necessary to maintain his optimum weight and condition. Your veterinarian can help you determine your dog's ideal weight.

If your dog leaves food in his dish, you are probably feeding too much. Conversely, if he gulps down his food and looks anxiously for more, you might be feeding too little. Offering food for only 15 minutes at each mealtime can help you to adjust the quantity you feed. If your dog does not eat his food, he might not be hungry. Try offering his meal at a later time. However, if your dog loses his appetite, especially for several days, he might be sick and should be taken to a veterinarian.

TIP

Fresh Food

To feed the freshest food, buy no more than one month's supply at a time and buy the food from a busy store whose inventory is constantly turned over.

Canned or Dry Food?

An adult can be fed both canned and dry food. Plaque and tartar will build up more quickly on the teeth of dogs fed only canned food. Consequently, their teeth will need dental cleaning more often.

Monitoring your dog's weight can help you determine if you are feeding the proper amount of food.

TIP

Chocolate

Chocolate is toxic to dogs. Be sure to keep any out of your dog's reach. It does not take much for a small dog to be poisoned.

Feeding Etiquette

Dogs like schedules and do best when fed around the same time each day. Some dogs prefer to eat their meal in a quiet part of the house; others are not bothered by a lot of activity. Some dogs become protective of their food dish and the area in which they are fed, but it is unacceptable for a dog to growl or lunge at anyone who walks by or up to the dog while he is eating. Your dog should "sit" and "stay" for his meal, and eat only when released. Hand-feeding your puppy some of his food during his mealtimes can help prevent food-guarding behavior from developing. Consult a dog trainer if your puppy or adult dog shows aggressive behavior when fed.

Drinking Water

Make sure that your dog always has clean, fresh water. If your dog spends time both indoors and out, he should have water bowls in both locations. Water bowls need to be washed at least every few days. A slime can coat the bowls, which will not be removed by simply emptying and refilling with water.

The Finicky Eater

Small-breed dogs have a reputation for being refined, finicky eaters. However, like all dogs, small breeds do not need variety and do perfectly well on one brand of premium food all their life. Small dogs have the same nutritional needs as larger breeds, but they just eat more per pound because they have a higher metabolism. Owners create their own finicky eaters. You are more likely to end up with a fussy eater by feeding your dog a variety of foods while he is young. Some people enjoy catering to their dog's taste, which is fine if they rely on different flavors of premium dog foods. However, when table scraps are substituted for regular meals, a dog's diet and health suffer.

Table Scraps

Many owners of small dogs do enjoy sharing table scraps with their dog. As long as table scraps do not comprise more than 10 percent of your dog's diet, they are unlikely to cause any problems. However, when table scraps regularly comprise more than 25 percent of your dog's diet, problems such as obesity and

Scheduled meal times will help with house-training.

Dinner Bones

Small dogs enjoy chewing bones. Gnawing on bones massages a dog's gums and helps to clean his teeth by scraping off tartar and other debris; however, do *not* feed your dog any kind of bone from your leftover meals. In particular, never offer any type of poultry bone, which can splinter. While a bone splinter might get stuck in your dog's throat, the more common hazard is internal damage such as punctured intestines. Bone splinters can seriously injure a dog's digestive tract; large bone chunks can be swallowed and cause blockages. Chewing on hard bones is a common cause of fractured teeth. Although veterinary dentists can now perform root canals for dogs, it is an expensive option for a preventable problem.

unbalanced nutrition can occur. Many people object to feeding scraps because they believe it encourages their dog to beg. However, if the dog is not fed directly from the table, and is kept out of the dining area during meals, begging should not be a problem.

Some types of table scraps can cause digestive upset in sensitive dogs, resulting in gas or diarrhea. Because of this possibility, do not feed your puppy any table scraps until after he is house-trained. High-fat foods, such as potato chips, are particularly likely to cause such problems. Use good judgment if you choose to feed your dog leftovers.

Treats

Treats are a pleasant way to indulge your dog, a useful tool for training, and convenient when traveling. Treats made for dogs are less likely to

═══════ TIP ═══════

Weighing Your Dog

Once your small dog is fully grown, weighing him is the easiest way to keep track of his weight. Weigh yourself, then weigh yourself while holding your dog, and calculate the difference between the two weights.

cause digestive problems than most people food. Some varieties are high in calories so do not overindulge your dog. Choose wisely—some treats are poor-quality junk food with dyes and preservatives. If you are using treats to train your dog, reduce the amount of his regular ration or else use his regular food for training treats.

The Overweight Dog

A dog is considered obese when he is 20 percent or more above his normal weight. Excessive weight puts a dog at increased risk for chronic health problems. It is always easier to prevent your dog from becoming overweight than it is to put him on a diet. Reduced-calorie foods are available for overweight dogs. Consult a veterinarian before putting your pet on a reducing diet.

An overweight dog also needs more exercise. Be sure other family members know they are not to feed any meals or treats without your permission. If you think your dog is overweight and you are feeding him properly, or you have put him on a reducing diet but he still does not lose weight, he should be examined by your veterinarian.

TRAINING AND SOCIALIZATION

Your puppy does not know the rules, and must be taught how to behave and what is right and wrong. Training is how you communicate with him. Patience, consistency, and a pleasant attitude will make training rewarding for both you and your puppy.

Your puppy might fit in the palm of your hand, but just like his large-breed relatives, he has the desire and intelligence to learn. Training is the best insurance to help guarantee you and your puppy a happy life together. Behavior problems are one of the main reasons people give up their dogs. Your commitment to training reduces the likelihood of this happening to you and your dog. Should circumstances ever arise that require you to find a new home for your small dog, it will be much easier to do if he is trained and socialized.

Training lets your puppy know what is expected of him. Dogs that are trained are secure and confident because they know where they fit in a family's structure and in human society. Knowing what is and is not allowed enhances a dog's self-confidence.

A well-trained dog will respond to your commands in a variety of situations.

Positive Reinforcement

Positive treatment and reinforcement of desired behaviors is the best method to use to train your small dog. This method uses praise such as a small, pea-sized tidbit of food or your voice, and correction, not punishment, to achieve the desired behavior. Some people are against using food treats because they think their puppy should understand and execute a command because he loves them. But a puppy will work harder if he gets a good reward, just like you do when you are paid with money for a job well done.

Proper use of food treats is important. When first learning a command, immediately praise and give a food treat when your puppy has done what you wanted. Once your puppy has solidly learned a command, you will switch and randomly reward him with the treat or praise. Your puppy will perform his best if he does not know when to expect a treat or praise. As his

that it is easier to prevent problems than it is to fix them. Direct and encourage behaviors that are desirable for an adult dog; do not encourage behaviors that will be difficult to tolerate in an adult. Begin teaching your puppy to get used to being touched all over, including his mouth, ears, and feet.

repertoire of commands increases, you will reward him with a food treat only for learning new commands, not for performing the ones he should already know. Eventually, you will not use food treats at all. For more complicated commands, a chance to play a game of "Fetch" might be an effective reward for some dogs.

Training Equipment

A flat buckle collar is sufficient for your puppy's training. In addition a 6-foot (1.8-m) leash or a retractable leash, between 10- to 15-feet (3- to 5-m) long is needed. The longer leash help you to practice and enforce obedience commands when your puppy is further away from you. Some smooth-coated breeds, such as Dachshunds, can slip out of their collars and a harness works better.

When to Begin Training

Begin training as soon your puppy enters your home. As long as you are clear and consistent about what is and is not allowed, your puppy will learn. A basic rule of dog training is

Short Sessions

Puppies have a short concentration time. Keep your training sessions short and integrate numerous short sessions into daily life. For example, tell your puppy to sit before each meal. When working on a command, do not practice for so long that your puppy loses interest and is bored. Executing a command two to three times is often enough. Always end a training session on a positive note while your puppy is still interested and has performed a command well.

Train your puppy when he is on his best behavior and when he is ornery—obedience is not just limited to your puppy's good times. Work with your puppy to build his confidence and trust in your authority. As your puppy matures, training sessions can lengthen and incorporate more commands.

Tone of Voice

Your tone of voice should reflect your leadership role.

✔ Firmly give a command only once.

✔ Avoid giving commands such as *"Come on—sit down."* Your commands should be clear and concise and the puppy should have no doubt what you mean (for example, *"Sit"* or *"Down"*).

✔ Use one-word commands.

✔ Do not whine, cajole, or plead, *"Please, come on—sit down."* This tone of voice can communicate distress to your dog since it sounds like whimpering; at the very least it is not clear and forceful.

✔ Change the tone of your voice when you give a verbal correction. If your puppy still does not respond, issue the correction in a low, firm tone.

Timing

When to give praise or a correction is very important. In order for your puppy to associate his behavior with your response, your praise or correction must be given when his behavior is occurring (within three seconds!). Dogs do not have a human conception of time. Your dog will not remember that five minutes ago he was chewing a shoe; therefore, he will not associate your anger with his previous actions. However, in response to your upset demeanor (even if you think you are not giving out any signals), he will lower his body and eyes and put back his ears, giving the appearance of guilt. Most animal behaviorists agree that dogs do not feel guilt, spite, or other negative human emotions that are often attributed to them, most notably when they have misbehaved.

Puppy Stages

Your puppy will not always think you are wonderful and fascinating. For the first few weeks, your puppy will naturally want to stay close to you, but within a few weeks, he will be more confident and independent, at which point he might hesitate before deciding whether to respond to your commands.

Teaching your puppy to establish eye contact with you can help to keep his attention focused on you. Eye contact is a form of dominance. Do not "lose" by being the first to break eye contact. Using a small food treat held near your eyes, tell your puppy, *"Watch me"* and reward him when he looks in your eyes. Eventually, move the treat away from your face, and reward your puppy with it when he looks in your eyes, not at the treat.

A well-socialized small dog enjoys meeting new people.

The Leader

You must take the leadership role with your small dog. If you do not, your dog will have you living according to his terms, not yours. As your puppy matures, and in particular, when he is an adolescent, he will occasionally try to challenge your authority. You must not ignore his challenges. To many people, these challenges can be subtle, but most start with the ignored command.

Never give your dog a command that you are not prepared or able to enforce. This means you do not "lazily" request your dog to sit, and when he does not comply, you ignore his disobedience. It takes a certain energy and alertness to enforce a command. If you are not going to follow

This Boston Terrier enjoys performing tricks.

through, do not give your puppy a command. You must know before you give a command that you mean it. Such situations occur less frequently in a structured setting, such as obedience class or when you are practicing your puppy's lessons. They are most likely to happen within your home when you are busy and distracted. This is when it matters most, because this is how your puppy will share your home.

As your puppy's leader, you must be consistent and persistent and enforce your commands and rules. Doing so can be hard work, but is ultimately worth it. You must be alert and pay attention to your puppy, even when you are tired or your puppy's misbehavior is cute. Sometimes it will seem easier to ignore half-bad behavior than to correct it; however, arbitrarily enforcing rules will confuse your puppy and can lead to his testing your authority.

Obedience Classes

Formal classes are invaluable. Your puppy learns basic obedience and good manners; you learn how to train your puppy. Either regular obedience classes or puppy kindergarten classes, which tend to be less structured, are suitable. Finding an instructor who provides a safe environment for puppies of all sizes is important as the boisterous play of larger puppies can be dangerous for tiny puppies. Ideally, your instructor should have experience training small-breed dogs. The benefits of a good obedience class include the assistance of someone experienced in working with a wide variety of dogs and situations. Make sure the instructor requests proof that all canines are either vaccinated or on a vaccination schedule. An instructor is invaluable when you run into a problem

*Always supervise young children
and small dogs.*

and cannot figure out how to solve it. Instead of feeling aggravated, the instructor can help you remedy the situation.

Consistent Control

Always train your puppy on a leash so that you have control over him. Without a leash you have no way of enforcing your commands, and your puppy might get bored and walk away or realize that he does not have to listen to you. The only way a puppy learns to obey commands is to realize that once given, commands that have been learned must be obeyed. Give a command only once before gently enforcing it. You want your puppy to respond to *"Stay,"* not to *"Stay, stay, stay."* Once your puppy responds reflexively to your commands in a variety of situations and circumstances, then you can begin to practice each command off leash.

Different breeds of small dogs have different aptitudes for learning. Some breeds will learn a command after a few repetitions. Other breeds will take considerably longer—days, or even weeks. How reliably your dog performs a command can also vary. Some breeds forget more easily than others. Some puppies get bored with repetition and will tune you out. Training in a variety of environments can help.

Commands

The Command "No!"

Inevitably, your puppy will learn the command *"No!"* shortly after he comes into your

home. Do not frighten your puppy into learning this command. Just say it loud enough for him to hear, and then give him something else to do, or put him out of harm's way. Avoid overusing this command; your puppy should not think his name ends or begins with *"No."* If you see your puppy heading toward mischief, head him off and give him something acceptable to do.

Release Command

Of absolute importance is a release command, which can be *"Release!"* or *"Break!"* This command lets your puppy know that he can break the previous command and resume doing what he wants. Many owners make the mistake of telling their dog to sit or lie down and then they forget about him. Eventually, the dog gets up and moves. Sometimes, the owner yells at the dog for moving, but other times the owner ignores the dog. This inconsistency is confusing to the dog. Therefore, never give a command without also knowing that you want your dog

to break it only when you "release" him. For example, when you command your puppy to sit, you will let him know he can get up from the *sit* when you give the release command. If at first your puppy does not seem to understand the release command, get him excited and he will break his position.

Socialization

Socialization is very important for small-breed dogs because owners tend to be overprotective, which can eventually encourage antisocial behavior. Socialization occurs when you expose your puppy to new environments, such as parks, shops, noisy school yards, and friends' homes, and you introduce him to as many new people as possible of all ages and sizes. As long as he is calm and happy, socialization helps your puppy learn to get along with others and provides him with positive experiences so he does not become shy or fearful. Socialization will help to prevent potential

Socialization is an important part of training.

future problems and is as important for your dog as basic obedience training.

Because of the risk of infection to a puppy that has not completed his vaccinations, check with your veterinarian as to the safest age to take your puppy to new places. You should continue to socialize your puppy as he grows and matures. Whatever might be part of your puppy's future life, he should meet while he is young. Do let him meet friendly dogs who have current vaccinations.

Keep your puppy on a leash during these excursions for safety and control. Make your excursions positive experiences. Reassure your puppy if he becomes scared, but do so with happy, bold words to encourage his confidence. Do not feed his fear by cooing. Seek socialization situations for your puppy while he still young. If you do not have children, take your puppy to a park on the weekend. Let him smell, see, and hear children running and playing. This exercise is especially important if you think there are children in your future or they are part of your extended family. Most people like meeting puppies and young dogs. Parents will bring their children to visit you or a child might ask if he can pet your puppy.

Since a puppy is irresistible, have some small pieces of dog biscuit a child can offer to your puppy while he is sitting. Be prepared to correct the puppy if he tries to jump or gets unruly. Because young puppies still have sharp teeth and might grab, the child can offer the treat on a flat hand. Children and adults are usually receptive and patient if you tell them your puppy is in training and is learning how to behave properly.

Participating in fun activities with your dog contributes to an enjoyable life for both of you.

HOW–TO: BASIC OBEDIENCE

"Sit," "Down," "Stay," "Come," "Heel," and *"Give"* are the six simple obedience commands that every dog needs to know in order to make him a pleasant companion with whom to share your life. The following methods of teaching the basic commands work well and you are certainly encouraged to follow up with additional commands that can be found in training books and through local dog clubs.

Sit

Many puppies quickly learn this command after only a few repetitions. Show him a treat, then raise it above his head so that he naturally moves into the sitting position. When he does, say *"Sit"* and give the treat. Have him sit for a few seconds, then give your release command so

Practice the "Sit" command in different locations.

he can get up. When you have his attention again, repeat the lesson. If your puppy tries to get up before the release command, gently tap his hindquarters with your finger so he sits again. Praise him, then release him.

Down

Once your puppy knows how to sit, you can teach him *"Down."* This is a difficult command for some puppies because it puts them in a subordinate position and can make them feel vulnerable. First, have your puppy sit. Then show him a treat and move the treat down and forward until it is near his chest and the ground. The puppy should move into the *down* position. When he does, say *"Down"* and reward him. If necessary, gently tap his shoulders with one finger. He can get back up after you give the release command.

Stay

Many small dogs bred as companions find this command difficult and an affront to their sensibilities since they prefer to always be at your side. You will teach your puppy the command *"Stay"* while he is in the *down* position and after he has mastered *"Sit"* and *"Down."* Command

your puppy, *"Down,"* then put your palm forward, in front of his face and say *"Stay."* Stand up and step back a few paces. Move slowly and wait a few seconds before returning to your puppy. Put your foot on the leash so your puppy cannot jump up when you get closer. Praise your puppy for staying, give him a treat, and then release him.

If your puppy gets up before you release him, put him back in the *down* position without scolding and start again. Gradually increase the distance you go from your puppy. After he *stays* with you standing in front of him, slowly circle around him. Hold the leash and let it slide through your hand so you can exert pressure should your puppy try to get up. An instructor is useful when you are teaching *"Stay"* and increasing your distance from your puppy. If your puppy tries to follow you, the instructor can quickly correct him. (The puppy might perceive you running back to correct him as a reward for breaking his *stay.*)

Come

"Come" means your dog quickly comes directly to you. This is an essential command that can save your dog's life

and save you from yelling yourself hoarse. It is very important that when you teach this command you are able to enforce it. When starting a training program, do not use *"Come"* if you cannot make your puppy respond. Give the command only if you have a 6-foot (1.8-m) or a retractable leash attached to your puppy. Give the command only once, and if your puppy does not pay attention, reel him in with the leash. Open your arms, bend down, be enthusiastic and your puppy will respond. Lavishly praise or give a treat to your puppy for coming when called, then release him and repeat the exercise.

A few caveats

✔ Start training from short distances—for instance, 5 feet (1.5 m)—and progress to longer distances using the retractable leash; practice the command in a variety of situations.

✔ Once your puppy consistently responds to the command when he is on leash, you can practice training him off leash.

✔ Do not run after your puppy if he ignores you; instead call his name and slowly jog away from him (he cannot resist the invitation to pursue you).

✔ Call him only when there is a high likelihood that he will respond (such as when he is not doing something more interesting).

✔ Finally, never yell at him for (eventually) coming.

Heel

"Heel" is the command you will use to teach your puppy to walk on a loose leash, without pulling. Many owners of small breeds do not mind if their dogs charge ahead of them on the leash; because their dogs are small, the pulling is not too uncomfortable. Nevertheless, a well-mannered dog should know how to heel.

First, train your puppy to *"Line up"* on your left side. Standing in front of your puppy, use a

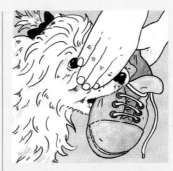

The command "Give" teaches the dog to give you whatever he has in his mouth.

food treat to move him behind your back and into a sitting position at your left side. Give the command *"Line up,"* tap your left thigh, and reward him.

From this position and using a short leash, purposely move forward with your left leg and give the command, *"Heel."* If your puppy bolts ahead of you, do a 180-degree turn and move in the opposite direction. Enough surprise turns will teach him that you are the leader and he has to pay attention and follow you. It is important that you never yank or spin your small puppy. Gently coax him in the right direction, and the correct position by your side, with a food treat. For best results, continue to practice this as your puppy grows and develops, and eventually train it in different locations.

Give

"Give" usually means your puppy delivers and places an object in his mouth into your hand. Practice *"Give"* with your puppy's bones and toys. As the leader, you have the right to take away your puppy's toys or chews. Calmly and gently say *"Give"* and firmly take away the object. Do not let your puppy grab it back. Praise your puppy and then give him back his toy or bone. Incorporating play, not a food treat, will reward your puppy for giving you the object.

GROOMING YOUR SMALL DOG

Do not wait until your puppy is almost grown to introduce the grooming process, as it will be more difficult for you and for the puppy.

Professional Grooming

Many small-breed dogs with long hair, as well as wire-coated breeds such as the Schnauzer, require professional grooming. The groomer you choose should require proof of vaccination for all canine clients. Plan on taking your puppy to the groomer after he has received his first shots.

Many groomers recommend that a puppy come in for several visits during the first week. The goal of the visits is not a cut and styled puppy, but to acclimate the puppy to the sights, sounds, and procedures. The groomer should be gentle, calm, and patient so the puppy has positive experiences. Even though your puppy will not be properly clipped, expect to pay full price for the groomer's time. You do not want the groomer to rush. The groomer will introduce the puppy to clippers and water, and begin to teach him how to stand on the

Long-haired breeds require more grooming compared to breeds with smooth coats.

grooming table. He or she should also show you how to perform maintenance grooming procedures at home.

Grooming at Home

Brushing

Smooth-coated breeds are referred to as wash-and-wear-dogs. Their short, smooth coat is easy to care for and does not require special brushing. A rubber brush or hound glove is ideal to help remove loose hair. Once or twice a week is sufficient to remove debris, dirt, and hair. A chamois leather cloth will give the coat a smooth shine. Mud is easily brushed off once it is dry.

Long-haired breeds should be softly brushed while your pet is still a puppy. A puppy's skin is more sensitive to touch than an adult's skin is. Start with a soft bristle brush, even if the puppy's coat will eventually require a wire slicker or pin brush. Make sure you do not hurt

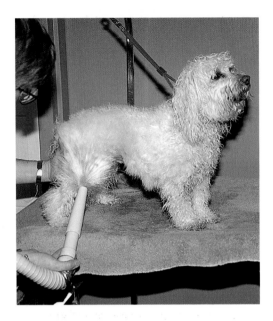

Plan on introducing your dog to professional grooming while still a puppy.

Grooming should be a pleasant experience for your dog.

your puppy while you are brushing him. If you must comb out hair mats, take your time and consider cutting out tough mats. Hurting your puppy or dog while brushing can cause him to become fearful of being touched.

Learning to tie up the hair of the crown takes a bit of practice. First, on each side, make a part running from the eye to the ear. Then fasten the strands with a rubber band and a barette.

Note: Don't forget to regularly comb and brush hanging ears that are covered with hair, as the hair becomes matted very easily, especially behind the ears.

Bathing

Short-haired breeds need to be bathed only as necessary, which can be a couple of times a year or as infrequently as once a year. Long-haired breeds tend to get their coats dirty more quickly; consequently, they need baths more often. Some small dogs can be washed in the sink, while others need to be put in the bathtub. Use warm water and a mild dog shampoo sold at pet stores. Be careful not to get shampoo in your dog's eyes or ears when lathering and rinsing the shampoo. After thoroughly rinsing your dog, rub him dry with a towel and keep him inside and away from drafts.

TIP

Ear Mites

Ears that are continually dirty could indicate an infection or an infestation with ear mites, which are transmitted from other dogs. If your dog's ears smell bad, look irritated, or have a discharge, he needs to be immediately examined by a veterinarian.

Clean the outer portion of your dog's ears every few weeks.

Note: Most dogs do not like baths, no matter how warm the water. Giving your dog an occasional bath while he is still young will get him used to the experience.

Ear Care

You should make it a habit to check your dog's ears every week. For dogs with hanging ears and breeds with a heavy growth of hair, checking the ears weekly is essential. Keeping the ears clean of debris will help prevent them from becoming smelly, and possibly infected. For many dogs, wiping the outer part clean with cotton balls will suffice. Any wax or debris further down the ear can be carefully removed using a special solution available from your veterinarian. Do not use cotton swabs in your dog's ear canal, which is beyond the area you can easily see—doing so can seriously injure your dog's ear.

Usually, if your dog gets something in his ear, such as a grass seed, he will shake or scratch at his head or carry his head at a tilt. Teaching your dog to allow you to examine his ears while he is still a puppy is useful as you might be able to remove the offending object yourself. How-ever, if you cannot see anything in your dog's ear, you must take him to a veterinarian.

Long-haired breeds often need to have the hair plucked or trimmed from the inside of their ears. Otherwise, the hairs inside the ears can become matted with earwax and dirt. This can lead to a moist environment where bacteria or yeast can thrive, which will result in an ear infection. For that reason, have your veterinarian or groomer show you how to pluck or trim the ear hair; or you can have them do it.

Dental Care

Small dogs suffer disproportionately from dental problems, including periodontal disease, abscesses, and tooth decay and loss. To prevent these conditions, a dog's teeth need dental care. Teeth covered with tartar and inflamed gums can cause more than bad breath: the bacteria can travel from infected teeth and gums to the dog's heart and kidneys, causing a serious infection in these organs. Bones, such as rawhides and nylabones, and hard crunchy foods can help prevent tartar from accumulating on your dog's teeth.

Milk Teeth

Keep a close eye on a growing puppy whose milk teeth should fall out by about six months of age. Sometimes, puppy teeth do not fall out at the right time; the permanent teeth then grow in crooked behind the milk teeth. If the milk teeth are still too firmly lodged, they have to be extracted by a veterinarian.

While you can teach your puppy to let you clean his teeth, noticeable tartar does not usually accumulate on a dog's teeth until he is one to three years old. Nonetheless, slowly begin teaching your puppy to let you brush his teeth so that he will learn to accept it; some dogs grow to love it. To prevent tartar buildup, clean your dog's teeth once a week or if necessary, daily.

You can remove tartar with a variety of products including a soft toothbrush and dog toothpaste, tooth scalers and scrapers, and

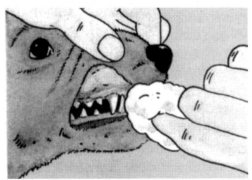

Dental wipes can help prevent tartar.

dental cleaning wipes. Brushing your dog's teeth at least once a week with a soft toothbrush and dog toothpaste will help keep them free of plaque and tartar. Do not use human toothpaste, which will cause stomach upset since dogs cannot spit out the toothpaste. Scalers and scrapers can be used less often. Always scrape away from the dog's gum line. These sharp tools can cut your dog if used incorrectly. Many pet owners find dental cleaning wipes that wrap around the finger easiest to use. However, to be effective, the wipes should be used every day.

Professional Cleaning: Because it is difficult to clean at the gum line, a professional cleaning is eventually necessary. In particular, a heavy tartar buildup usually needs to be removed by a veterinarian while your dog is sedated. The results will help keep your dog's teeth strong and healthy and keep his breath from smelling bad. Depending on the dog, a professional cleaning might be needed once every six months or once every two years. Your veterinarian can recommend how often your dog's teeth should be professionally cleaned.

Eye Care

Regularly check your dog's eyes. Small dogs get a larger share of dust on walks than do bigger breeds. The dust lodges in the corners of their eyes and can cause an eye infection if not removed. While dogs sleep, eye secretions frequently collect, and these also have to be removed.

Some small-dog breeds, for example, the King Charles Spaniel, have large protruding eyes that tear easily. Their eyes should be cleaned regularly; otherwise, the tears will leave an unsightly stain on the hair just under the eyes. In dogs with white coats, such as the Maltese, these stains can be removed with eye cleaning preparations sold in pet stores or by groomers. Excessive tearing requires immediate treatment by a veterinarian.

Nail Care

Your small dog's nails probably will not wear down naturally, even if you walk him on hard surfaces, so you will need to cut them. Plan on beginning while your puppy is still young. Young puppies rarely put up a fight when first having their nails clipped, but older puppies and dogs do. If you can hear your dog's nails click against a hard floor, or if the nails touch the floor surface, they are probably too long and should be trimmed. Overgrown nails can snag and tear. A torn nail is painful and can become infected.

Dewclaws: Use small sharp nail clippers to cut the nail below the quick, which is the portion that contains the nails' blood supply and nerves. Some breeds have their dewclaws removed. Dewclaws are functionless claws on the inside of the front feet that do not reach the ground when walking. If your dog still has his dewclaws, it is important that you also trim them regularly.

The quick: If your dog's nails are light-colored you can see the dark line or quick. Shining a flashlight at the nail will sometimes help to illuminate the quick. You can also have your dog lie on his back and examine the nails from underneath to determine where the quick is located. A nail's quick will grow out as the nail lengthens. If you wait too long between periods of nail cutting, you will have to gradually cut

Protect your pets by keeping them on a leash in busy areas.

TIP

Cutting the Quick

By trimming off small portions at a time rather than making one large cut, you are less likely to accidentally cut the quick, which is painful to your dog and can make him wary of future nail cutting. If you do draw blood, apply pressure with a wet cloth for three to five minutes to stop the bleeding. You can also apply a commercial clotting powder to the end of the nail to stop the bleeding.

the tips back over a period of days and weeks to return the nails to a healthy length.

When teaching a puppy to allow his nails to be clipped, be slow and patient. Snip just a little off of each nail, or cut just one or two nails a day if necessary. Make it a low-key, positive experience. The best time to cut his

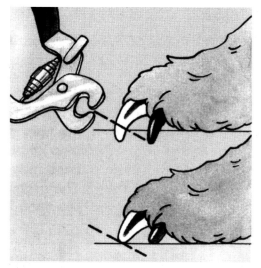

When trimming your pet's nails, make sure you don't injure the quick.

nails is after he has had a vigorous play session, not when he is wound up and ready to go. Praise him after you cut his nails, but not so much that he becomes overexcited.

Trimming nails is difficult for many pet owners. Dogs don't particularly like to have their feet fussed with, so learning the correct way from the beginning will save time and keep you and your dog happier. Even if you plan to leave the task of nail trimming to a dog groomer or veterinarian, practice touching, holding, and examining your puppy's feet so that he will learn not to mind having his feet handled.

Foot Care

Check your dog's feet after he has been outdoors. Chewing gum that gets stuck between the toes is no disaster, but foxtails or splinters

Many long-haired breeds require professional grooming.

A well-groomed dog is picture perfect.

Sometimes it can be difficult to keep a white dog's coat clean.

of glass can cause pain and infection. For long-haired breeds, keep the hair between the toes from getting too long. Carefully trim the hair with scissors or clippers. Keeping the hair short will also reduce the amount of dirt your dog tracks into the house. After walking on snowy city streets, remove any clumps of snow and clean your dog's paws to prevent salt from irritating the pads.

Care of the Rear

For long-haired breeds, occasionally checking the rear end is necessary. Sometimes feces get matted around the hair near the anus. Besides being unhygienic, it can also promote infections in this area. Keeping the hair trim near the anus can prevent this potential problem. A dog has two anal glands or sacs, which are normally emptied by pressure during defecation. The glands' scent is probably used for marking territory and likely accounts for why dogs sniff each other's rear end. If your dog scoots around the floor on his hind end, his anal sacs might be impacted and blocked. Your veterinarian or groomer will have to express the sacs to remove the fluid. If this occurs regularly, your veterinarian might recommend a change in diet or show you how to remove the fluid.

Dogs are creatures of habit and adapt best to clear rules. Do not give your dog mixed messages. Knowing how to prevent undesirable behaviors will help your dog become a well-adjusted family member.

Behavior Problems

How do you turn your small dog into a stereotypic yapping, snapping little terror? Choose the path of least resistance—unconditionally accept whatever behavior your dog exhibits, and then make excuses for the behavior? Indulging your dog like this will lead to obnoxious behavior that you will soon grow weary of living with, or earn you the reputation for having a nasty little dog that no one else wants to be around. The longer you tolerate your dog's inappropriate behavior, the more likely the dog will learn that the behavior is acceptable—once the behavior becomes habitual, it will be much harder to break.

To a dog, there is no such thing as just once. He is either allowed on the bed and furniture, or he is not. Like people, dogs do not adapt as willingly or as well to rules that become more restrictive. For example, your dog will gladly learn to share your bed, but he is much less

Make sure that the toys you select are safe for small dogs.

willing to "unlearn" sharing your bed. Decide early what furniture, if any, your dog can share with you.

Barking

Many small breed dogs are excessive barkers. Given inadequate exercise and attention, they can develop into nuisance barkers that bark because they are lonely and bored. If you are not home during the day to correct this behavior, it can develop into a problem. If necessary, several anti-barking devices, such as collars that squirt citronella oil or administer a small shock, can be used to help stop barking. However, the underlying reasons for the barking (such as boredom), must be addressed. When you are at home, teaching your dog to bark and be quiet on command can be effective at controlling this behavior.

Jumping

Friendly dogs and puppies jump up on people as a form of greeting, especially when they are happy and excited. However, it can be annoying

Regular veterinary care is important for older dogs.

when your dog jumps up, especially if you are dressed nicely, or if your dog jumps on guests. As is true of most things, it is much easier to prevent this habit from developing in a puppy than it is to train an adult dog not to jump:

✔ Crouch down when greeting your puppy so he does not have to jump.

✔ Calmly greet your puppy; do not get excited upon seeing him.

✔ Redirect your puppy's enthusiasm by distracting him with something else, such as tossing one of his toys.

Because jumping up is self-rewarding, teach your puppy that jumping will be ignored. If he jumps on you, step back or turn aside so he cannot make contact, and ignore him until all four feet are on the ground. When your puppy jumps, firmly say *"No!"* Give the command *"Off!"* followed by the command *"Sit."* When he complies, praise him. Be persistent—teaching your dog not to jump can take a while.

Dominance Behavior

Your dog should never exhibit aggressive behavior, such as growling or snapping at you, a family member, or a friend. If your dog growls when asked to get off the couch or bed, or when a person wants to join him on the couch or bed, you have a problem. Teach your dog that he is allowed on and off the furniture on your command only. The first time he growls or snaps, he's off the bed and should be put in his crate to sleep. Dominance aggression occurs in situations where the dog believes he is in charge. It is typically directed at people the dog does not consider his equal.

Guarding behavior of a food dish, bone, or toy also should not be tolerated. Early lessons on relinquishing an object and sitting for meals can help prevent this behavior. Because small-breed dogs are less imposing than large ones, many pet owners try to ignore the behavior and avoid situations likely to provoke the dog's aggression.

If your dog exhibits dominance aggression, you need the help of a professional trainer—even small dogs can cause disfiguring bites. Your veterinarian should be able to refer you to a qualified trainer. Prevent dominance behavior by teaching your puppy to relinquish objects when asked and to not display guarding behavior. Obedience classes will also help.

Aggression Toward Other Dogs

Some small dogs go on the offensive, growling, snapping, and barking at larger dogs. If the big dog runs away, the little one pursues. While this might be amusing, it can lead to serious injury or death for the small dog if the larger one returns the attack. Just as you would not allow a large dog to challenge another dog to a fight, do not allow your small dog to engage in this behavior. Prevention is the best approach. Distract your dog from his behavior by using obedience commands such as *"Sit"* and *"Watch me"* or leave the area before any trouble can start.

Aggression from Other Dogs

Nothing can be quite as scary as having a large dog aggressively charge your small dog while he is walking on a leash. Picking up your dog to protect him will not always solve the problem as big dogs can jump. Yelling for the owner might not be effective as some people think it is amusing to see their big dog behave this way. Carrying and knowing how to use pepper spray can be effective. Alternatively, avoid walking in areas where there are untrained dogs owned by rude people or contact animal control.

Visitors and Growling

Some small dogs defend their primary caretaker's lap or arm as their personal territory. When a child or visitor approaches, the dog growls. Do not accept this behavior. If your dog growls, say *"No!"* and put him down. If he stops, you can pick him up again. Having the other person give the dog a treat while he's on the floor and then progressing to receiving a treat while being held can help correct this

Dog shows are a good place to see a variety of small breeds all at once.

behavior. If the dog growls while he is at your feet, tell him *"No!"* and put him in another room where he can still see you and your visitor. After a few minutes, let your dog out. If he does not growl or bark, have the visitor give him a treat for good behavior.

Running Away

Even if they are provided with enough daily walks, when given the opportunity some small breeds will bolt and explore the neighborhood. Other small dogs enjoy nothing more than ending a bout of off-leash play with a game of *"Chase,"* instead of responding to *"Come."* Working on the basic obedience command, *"Come,"* especially with treats and a long retractable leash, can help. Training your dog to sit before he is allowed out a door or gate can help you maintain control. Or you can accept these behaviors and not let your dog ever get loose, or you can train your dog to incorporate games of *"Chase"* with treats for coming to you throughout his off-leash play sessions.

Breeds with thin coats are less likely to enjoy long play sessions in the snow.

Separation Anxiety

When left alone, barking and destructive behavior are typical symptoms of a small dog with separation anxiety. While many small dogs bond closely with their owners and do not like being alone, they do not develop separation anxiety.

Introduce your puppy to separations by keeping them brief and varying the length of time so your puppy will not know how long he will be by himself. Make your departures and returns low key and your puppy will not feel anxious. Keeping your puppy in his crate for your absences is one method of preventing this behavior from developing.

For a dog that already has separation anxiety, the typical treatment involves desensitizing the dog to your leaving the house. Pretend you are leaving by picking up keys and coat and leaving for a few minutes and then returning. Next, wait outside the door a little longer and at the first sign of misbehavior open the door and yell *"No!"* and then leave. When your dog has been quiet, reenter the house and praise him. You will gradually work up to absences of several hours. If given adequate exercise and a routine schedule, separation anxiety will sometimes go away by itself. Try keeping your dog busy with an enjoyable activity while you are gone. Coat the inside of a hollow bone with peanut butter and then freeze the bone. Give the frozen treat to your dog before you leave; it will keep him occupied for a long time.

If necessary, medication can be used as a last resort for treatment of separation anxiety. Consult your veterinarian who can evaluate your dog. The prescribed medication can be used to break the cycle of separation anxiety,

Proper training will prevent your small dogs from ruling the roost.

with the ultimate goal of gradually weaning your dog off the medication.

House-training Accidents

Small dog breeds are known for lapses in house-training manners. What brings about such lapses? There may be several causes. First, have your veterinarian rule out any disease-related cause. The second possibility is that your dog is responding to a change in the home environment. It can take some detective work to determine what has caused the problem. In the meantime, reimplement all the house-training rituals you used originally to train your dog.

Some mature male small dogs suddenly begin to mark, or urinate, in the house. This is more likely with multiple male dog households and with intact males than with neutered males. Besides neutering, keeping the dog(s) confined to one part of the house when you are not home can control and minimize the problem.

Spaying and Neutering

Spaying refers to removal of the female dog's ovaries and uterus. The male dog is neutered, which refers to the removal of the male's testicles. Unless you plan to breed your dog as part of a conscientious breeding program, you should fix him or her. After this procedure, your dog's

Changes in your senior dog's appearance or activity level could indicate a health problem.

activity level and personality will not change. Puppies can be safely spayed before they reach puberty and doing so reduces the risk of reproductive disorders and cancers.

If you wait, be aware that many small-breed females show little bloody discharge during the first phases of heat. You might not realize your female is in season, but intact male dogs will know and they can mate with your female. This can result in a dangerous situation for your female if she is mated by a larger-breed dog that can hurt her. The mating can also result in puppies that are too large for her to whelp.

The Senior Dog

While large dogs are considered seniors at seven years of age, because of their long life span, small-breed dogs become seniors later, depending on their breed. Older dogs sleep longer and more deeply. They slow down and are less active. However, they must still receive regular exercise, such as leisurely walks around the block. A consistent, moderate exercise regime will help keep your dog's muscles toned, his joints flexible, and his bones strong.

Obesity

Because senior dogs are less active, their caloric intake must be correspondingly reduced to prevent weight gain. Obesity increases the risk of heart disease and puts more stress on the older dog's joints.

Teeth

An older dog that loses his appetite might need his teeth cleaned. Swollen gums and loose teeth can make eating painful. Anesthesia, which is required for professional cleaning, is riskier for older dogs, so be diligent about brushing your dog's teeth.

Grooming

Grooming tasks, such as brushing and nail trimming, should not be neglected. Because he is less active, nail trimming might need to be done more frequently. Older dogs sometimes smell "doggy" as they age. This can be due to a skin condition called seborrhea. Brushing and occasional baths will reduce the smell as will regularly washing his bedding. Problems with teeth, ears, urinary tract, and anal glands can also make an older dog smell. Unpleasant odors indicate a potential problem and your veterinarian should be consulted.

Stiff Joints

Older dogs used to sleeping on your bed will have more difficulty jumping on and off the bed. Attractive ramps are available that can help your dog climb onto the bed. Alternatively, place a thick foam, orthopedic bed designed to relieve the stress of arthritis and stiff joints next to your bed. This will give your senior dog a comfortable place to sleep while still feeling like part of the family. Many times the behavior changes that occur in old dogs are thought to be a natural consequence of old age. But your dog might also be suffering from a painful medical condition that cannot be readily detected by you.

Note: Your senior dog should have annual or biannual visits to the veterinarian. These wellness checks can help to detect some ailments in their early stages, such as the cataracts that cause cloudy eyes in older dogs. Conditions detected in their early stages can be treated more successfully than those found when they are in advanced stages.

A Second Dog

A puppy often revives an older dog's interest in life, but the decision to get a new "replacement" dog while your present dog is growing older requires a thoughtful assessment of your senior dog's personality and condition. Not all dogs welcome a puppy, particularly "people dogs" that were never dog-friendly to begin with. As discussed above, some medical conditions, such as arthritis, are painful, and make it less likely that your dog will enjoy playing with a puppy. In such cases, provide your senior dog a safe retreat from the boisterous attention of the puppy and do not allow the puppy to make your senior miserable with his rambunctious behavior.

Saying Good-bye

Most people hope their old dog passes peacefully away in his sleep. Some dogs do die this way, but most pet owners are faced with

the painful decision of whether or not to put their dog to sleep. It is a major decision that can be very difficult to make. Good medical care can prolong the life of a treasured dog, but it can also extend it to the point where your dog's best interests are no longer served. Your veterinarian can help you assess the quality of your dog's life, especially if your dog is being treated for a fatal disease, such as an inoperable tumor. The decision is easier to make when a dog has no chance of recovery and is in pain, but more ambiguous situations abound. Your instincts will help you to know when your dog is not happy and his pain overrides his ability to enjoy life. You will be able to endure your grief more easily when you and your family make the decision with love and care. Ask if your veterinarian is willing to come to your home for the procedure. The comfortable, familiar surroundings will make it easier for both you and your dog.

Older dogs should visit the veterinarian at least once a year.

MEDICAL PROBLEMS AND AILMENTS

Trust your instincts. If you think your dog is sick, he probably is and you should contact your veterinarian. Prompt veterinary care of a possible medical condition will lead to the best outcome.

Your dog should have an annual veterinary checkup. Besides planned visits, there are also the unexpected visits. Symptoms that indicate a visit to the veterinarian is necessary are lumps and bumps, behavior changes, and long bouts of vomiting, diarrhea, or constipation. Loss of appetite is also a sign that something is amiss. Dogs do not get colds. If your dog has symptoms of a cold, such as runny eyes and nose, something is wrong and he should be seen by a veterinarian. Very often, waiting to treat a condition makes the recovery process longer and costlier. If a medication your veterinarian gives you does not work, you need to go back for further assistance.

Your veterinarian will check your dog for any inherited disorders.

Vomiting and Diarrhea

At some point in his life, your dog will experience vomiting or diarrhea. Fortunately, most bouts pass quickly and do not require veterinary treatment. Vomiting can occur for minor reasons, such as eating something disagreeable or eating too fast, but it can also be a result of infection, internal parasites, or digestive diseases. Persistent vomiting is serious, and your dog should be seen by his veterinarian.

Loose or watery bowel movements might be the result of your dog having eaten something disagreeable or a minor intestinal upset. However, diarrhea is also a symptom of infectious diseases and other ailments. If the diarrhea persists for 48 hours and is accompanied by other symptoms, such as lack of appetite, vomiting, or fever, it can indicate a serious illness that requires veterinary care. Your dog should be examined by a veterinarian particularly if he seems to be getting worse, or if there is blood or mucus in his droppings. A dog can become dehydrated and lethargic from diarrhea that lasts for several days.

For both vomiting and diarrhea, treatment typically entails withholding food for 12 to 24 hours. This fast is followed by several small bland meals of cooked white rice with cooked chicken or hamburger for one or two days. Then return your dog to eating his regular food.

Human Medications

Never give your dog any human medications without first checking with your veterinarian. Several common medicines for people, such as acetaminophen (Tylenol), are toxic to dogs. Your veterinarian might recommend human over-the-counter medications for some ailments that affect your dog. For example, enteric-coated aspirin is given to reduce inflammation and relieve pain; Dramamine is used for car sickness; and Benadryl is suitable for allergic reactions to insect stings and spider bites. Your veterinarian will give you information on the correct dosage based on your dog's weight and the condition being treated.

Parasites

External Parasites

Parasites are organisms that survive by living and feeding on other organisms. Fleas, ticks, and mites are external parasites that live on or within a dog's skin. These pests are detrimental to a dog's health. Parasites can spread disease and even transmit other types of parasites to a dog. If left untreated, parasites can be a serious problem.

Fleas: Fleas are the most common parasites that affect dogs. Heavy flea infestations can cause anemia, and fleas are also vectors for tapeworms. Some dogs are highly allergic to fleas, which can cause a condition called flea allergy dermatitis or flea-bite allergy. A flea injects saliva when it bites, which causes severe skin irritation and scratching. For dogs with an allergy to fleas, one flea bite can drive them crazy and send them into a frenzy of chewing and scratching themselves. Dogs can get fleas from other dogs, cats, and wild animals. Areas where numerous dogs play, such as dog parks, can also be sources.

In the last decade, a new generation of sophisticated flea products was developed that made flea control more convenient, as well as safer and more effective. They are often called "spot-on" because a single drop of the product is applied to the back of your dog's neck, typically only once a month. Ask your veterinarian to advise you as to what product is safest to use, in particular for a puppy or an old dog, and your veterinarian can monitor your pet's health and the method's effectiveness.

Many pet owners prefer "natural" remedies for flea control. Unfortunately, herbal remedies such as vitamin B, garlic, and brewer's yeast are not effective against fleas. However, vacuuming your house, especially where your dog spends his time, and washing your dog's bedding at least once a week, are natural flea-control methods. Flea-combing your dog for a few minutes every day is also a natural way to give your dog some immediate relief from biting fleas. Flea combs are easy to use on a smooth-coated breed, but difficult on dogs with a long coat. The fleas get trapped in the fine teeth of the comb and can then be killed with your fingers or washed into a cup of water with bleach or detergent.

Ticks: Ticks are active mainly in spring and summer. Adult ticks have four pairs of legs and feed on blood. Ticks attach themselves to a dog with their mouthparts. Besides biting your dog, ticks can bite you and other family members. Ticks are a concern because they can transmit serious diseases to both dogs and people.

If you find a tick biting your dog, apply some alcohol to the tick with a cotton-tipped applicator. The tick will be dead in a few minutes. Using tweezers, grasp the tick as close to the skin as possible and pull steadily to remove it. You can examine a large tick after removal to assess whether you have removed the mouth parts with the tick. Dispose of the tick by flushing it down the toilet. If your dog becomes sick shortly after you removed a biting tick, consult your veterinarian. Treatment for tick-borne illnesses is most successful if diagnosis and treatment begins right away.

Mange mites: Mites are not seasonal and can affect your dog at any time of the year. For all types of mite infestations, veterinary diagnosis and treatment is required. A veterinarian will identify the type of mite by examining skin scrapings under a microscope. Sometimes mites cannot be found in the scrapings, but based on the dog's symptoms, treatment to eliminate mites will be given anyway. When needed, a veterinarian can also prescribe an anti-inflammatory medication to relieve the dog's itchy condition.

Internal Parasites

Roundworms, hookworms, tapeworms, and heartworms are the most common internal parasites that affect dogs. If undetected and left untreated, internal parasites can be a serious problem. Because the eggs of many species of internal parasites are shed in a dog's droppings, it is important to pick up your dog's droppings to limit potential sources of infestation. Part of a new puppy checkup entails bringing a stool sample that is checked for the eggs of internal parasites. Your veterinarian will recommend whether annual checks are necessary. For all cases of internal parasites, rely on your veterinarian to diagnose and treat the condition with a deworming medication.

Heartworms: Heartworms are transmitted from dog to dog by the bite of an infected mosquito. The mosquito swallows the larval heartworms, called microfilaria, when it bites an infested dog. The larvae are passed into another dog when the mosquito feasts again. The larvae develop in subcutaneous tissues, then they travel to their final destination, which is the dog's heart. Symptoms of dogs infected with heartworms include coughing, weight loss, and fatigue. Heartworms are dangerous because they can kill a dog. Treatment of a dog with adult heartworms requires intensive care and can be life-threatening, especially if a large number of adult worms are present in the heart.

Heartworm infection is preventable with the use of medication. The medication is easy to administer because dogs like the chewable tablet and the tablet needs to be given only once a month. Some of the spot-on flea control products available from your veterinarian will also prevent heartworm. Before starting the medication, a veterinarian will take a blood sample to be sure your dog is not already infected.

In some parts of the country, mosquitoes are active all year and a dog should be given heartworm preventive throughout the year. In other areas, mosquitoes are present for only a few months. A dog might need to be on the preventive for only as long as mosquitoes are active. If your dog goes off the preventive, some veterinarians prefer to retest before starting the medication again. If you travel to a region of the country where heartworms are present, ask your veterinarian about starting the treatment before and while you are visiting.

Immunizations

Vaccines are given to prevent your dog from getting infectious diseases. Most vaccines are designed to prevent viral infections. Vaccinations are necessary because no drug is totally effective at curing viral infections once they are established. The risk of these diseases has been effectively reduced by the widespread use of vaccination programs. Vaccinations are the best method to make sure your dog does not become infected with these deadly pathogens.

For the first few weeks of your puppy's life, the antibodies present in the colostrum (first milk) from the mother will protect the puppy. However, if the mother has not developed immunity, neither will the puppy. For protection against numerous infectious diseases, puppies are typically immunized against

- distemper
- hepatitis
- parvovirus
- parainfluenza
- coronavirus
- leptospirosis.

Referred to as the puppy series, the shots are usually administered over a period of two to four months. Your puppy's first inoculation might have already been administered by the breeder or it might need to be given by your veterinarian. Your veterinarian will provide you with a schedule for your puppy's vaccinations. After the series is complete, an adult dog receives an annual vaccine booster for these same diseases.

Viral vaccines are not always completely effective and even dogs that have been vaccinated might still be susceptible to the virus. Factors such as nutritional status, age, and general health of the dog affect vaccine efficacy. Your veterinarian can discuss any mitigating factors with you. In many cases, some vaccines provide immunity for several years, but most dogs still receive annual boosters. Instead of a yearly vaccination, some veterinarians perform annual blood tests (called titers) that measure the dog's level of immunity. Such tests are typically performed for dogs that previously experienced an adverse reaction to vaccination, or are at genetic or physiological risk for reactions. If the level of immunity to infectious agents is too low, the dog is given the necessary vaccination.

Vaccinations are available for several ailments, including kennel cough (*Bordetella*), giardia, a protozoa that affects the digestive system, and Lyme disease, which is transmitted by ticks. Your veterinarian can advise you whether other vaccinations are recommended for your puppy.

Heatstroke

Dogs are not very efficient at cooling themselves. Although dogs perspire from their feet, they mainly cool themselves by panting. As a dog pants, body heat evaporates from his mouth. If the heat does not dissipate fast enough, the dog's body temperature can rise to a dangerous level. Dogs with short muzzles such as the Boston Terrier, as well as those with short muzzles and thick coats such as the Pekingese, are particularly vulnerable to heatstroke

Heatstroke is caused by exposure to high temperatures. Exercise on hot days or being left inside a car on a warm day are the main causes of heatstroke. The temperature inside a car can quickly climb to intolerable levels, even when a car is parked in the shade with the windows open. Heatstroke can develop in only a few minutes and cause a dog's body temperature to soar. Signs of heatstroke include rapid noisy breathing, bright red gums, a red enlarged tongue, and thick or excessive saliva. The dog's eyes may be glazed and he will be listless. In some cases, the dog vomits and has diarrhea. As the condition progresses, the dog's pulse will be rapid and weak, followed by shock, coma, and death.

Heatstroke is a medical emergency. A dog with heatstroke can die if he is not quickly cooled. Prevention of heatstroke is vital. During hot weather, resist the urge to take your dog with you in the car, even for short errands. If you must travel in hot weather with your dog, be prepared with a cooler of ice water and some ice packs. Even so, you still must not leave him unattended in the car.

Pet Health Insurance

Veterinary medicine is becoming more sophisticated and also costly. In cases of catastrophic illness or accident, pet health insurance can be a lifesaver for owners who might otherwise have to put down their dog because they could not afford his medical treatment. Like health insurance for people, pet insurance is based on a dog's age and has waiting periods for policies to take effect, deductibles, pay-out limits per incident, and exclusions. Policies might not cover congenital and hereditary illnesses or preexisting conditions, and might provide extremely limited coverage for older dogs. Ask your veterinarian for suggestions on a plan. Be sure to research your options before selecting a plan.

Finally, buy and read a good reference book on dog health and veterinary care. The book will help to answer your questions and provide a better understanding of your dog's health.

BREED PROFILES

The following descriptions do not necessarily reflect the official AKC breed standards and may differ from them in certain respects. However, the information provided on each breed's appearance and temperament will help you select the most suitable breed for your family.

Affenpinscher

The smallest member of the family of Pinschers and Schnauzers, the Affenpinscher originated in Germany in the 1600s. An impish miniature that proved itself as a catcher of rats and mice, Affenpinschers were also used on quail and rabbits.

Appearance: A wreath of hair frames his round little face with a prominent forehead. The muzzle is short, but not upturned as in the similar-looking Miniature Griffon. Its teeth often protrude somewhat. The eyes are round. It has busy, bristly eyebrows and cropped erect ears or natural ears. Its body is stocky and compact.

Height: 9–11.5 inches (23–28 cm)

Weight: 7–9 pounds (3.2–4.1 kg)

Coat and color: The Affenpinscher has a dense coat that is hard, lusterless, and shaggy.

Grooming: The coat needs to be brushed several times a week. The Affenpinscher needs

Each breed has a unique appearance and behavior.

to be trimmed periodically to maintain its typical appearance.

Temperament: The Affenpinscher can be bright and full of life, but occasionally also placid. Lovable, inclined to play jokes, and truly devoted, it is very attached to its home. Despite its diminutive stature, it makes a good watchdog.

Exercise: Daily walks outside are necessary.

Bichon Frise

Portraits from past centuries provide evidence that there was a Bichon in almost every aristocratic household of France and Italy. This little dog was the lady of the house's constant companion and served as a bed warmer at night.

Appearance: The dense, abundant coat makes this dog's appearance unmistakable. Round, dark eyes and a black nose are the only points of contrast on the light-colored head, which seems large because of the coat of hair.

Height: 9–11.5 inches (23–28 cm)

Weight: 7–12 pounds (3.2–5.4 kg)

The Affenpinscher was first bred in Germany.

Bichon Frise are charming and intelligent dogs.

Coat and color: The Bichon's hair is fine and soft, very thick and curled in loose corkscrews. The adult's hair is about 3 to 4 inches (7.6–10 cm) long. White is the only color.

Grooming: The Bichon should be gently brushed every day and any tangles removed. The ends of the coat can be cut to shape the coat. Professional grooming is recommended every few months. The eyes must be cleaned daily to prevent tears from discoloring the hair.

Temperament: Besides the Bichon's attractive powderpuff appearance, this breed's charm, intelligence, and merry attitude have contributed to its popularity. It also enjoys cuddling. Bichons are easygoing and are not typically aggressive toward people or other dogs.

Exercise: Bichons love exercise, and enjoy relatively long walks; hikes are not a problem. With daily walks, the Bichon is content in an apartment.

Boston Terrier

The Boston Terrier is the result of a cross between English Bulldogs and white English Terriers. The breed was officially recognized in the United States in 1893.

Appearance: The round head with the blocky muzzle is reminiscent of a Bulldog. The proud attitude and athletic body were inherited from the terriers. Because of their short muzzle, some Bostons wheeze and snore, and many don't tolerate heat well.

Height: 15–17 inches (38–43 cm)

Weight: 10–25 pounds (4.5–11.3 kg)

Coat and color: The hair is short, smooth, glossy, and fine textured. The color can be brindle, black, or seal with white markings. Seal appears black with a red cast when seen in bright light.

The Boston Terrier looks dashing in black and white.

Grooming: The coat needs only occasional brushing when the dog is shedding. The large eyes sometimes need daily cleaning.

Temperament: This imposing little dog is gentle, devoted, and sensitive to its owner's moods. It is calm and well mannered in the house. Consistent training is important for the clever Boston. It is a good watchdog. Like many small breeds, it can sometimes bark a lot. It is not fearful or aggressive toward people, but can sometimes be aggressive with other dogs.

Exercise: An athletic dog that needs an athletically inclined owner. The Boston needs daily walks and enjoys playing and chasing balls.

Brussels Griffon

Developed in Belgium in the 1800s, the Griffon was used to hunt rodents and provide companionship.

Appearance: With its long whiskers and beard, and a nose set deeply between the eyes, the Brussels has an almost human expression.

Although the Brussels Griffon can look ill-humored, it is friendly and affectionate by nature.

Although it has an undershot jaw, the lower teeth do not show when the mouth is closed. It has a thick, short body and is somewhat square in appearance. The tail is docked.

Height: 7–8 inches (17.8–20 cm)

Weight: 8–10 pounds (3.6–4.5 kg)

Coat and color: The rough coat is wiry and dense. The head is covered with longer wiry hair that forms a fringe around the face. Four colors occur: red, beige, black and tan, and black.

Grooming: Regular brushing and combing are necessary. The large eyes and folds of skin around the nose should be kept clean.

The Cairn Terrier was once used for hunting.

Temperament: Griffons are extremely devoted to their owners. In the home, the confident Griffons are high spirited, lively, and very alert. They adapt to their family and get along well with other dogs. With strangers, they tend to be reserved and cautious. Because Griffons bark infrequently and are not loud, they are well suited as apartment dogs. Hot or humid weather causes problems for these short-nosed dogs. They tend to snore and have a long life expectancy.

Exercise: The spunky Griffon needs to run and romp about. But it can usually get enough exercise with an indoor game of catch or a short walk on a leash.

Cairn Terrier

This breed originated in western Scotland during the Middle Ages. It was used to hunt foxes, badgers, and other vermin, for which it needed courage and perseverance.

Appearance: The wire coat looks natural and unsophisticated. Its short legs enabled it to go underground after its quarry.

Height: 11–12 inches (28–31 cm)

Weight: 16 pounds (7.5 kg)

Coat and color: The weather-resistant double coat consists of a harsh, long outer coat and a short, soft, furry undercoat. Except for white, any color is acceptable. Red, gray, sand, and wheat are the most common colors.

Grooming: Regular brushing and combing are required. The dead hairs need to be professionally stripped from the coat twice a year.

Temperament: The spirited Cairn can be a bundle of energy, undaunted by the hustle and bustle of large families. Affectionate and independent, the clever and inquisitive Cairn is still fond of cuddling at appropriate times. Its urge to hunt is still present and you need to train it firmly to maintain your authority over it.

Exercise: Daily walks or games in the yard are required.

Cavalier King Charles Spaniel

This small spaniel had spaniel hunting dogs as ancestors. It originated in England in the 1600s and was a favorite among royal households. By the beginning of the twentieth century the breed had almost become extinct. Today, however, it is becoming more popular every year in the United States.

Appearance: An elegant little dog with large eyes and fringed drooping ears.

Height: 12–13 inches (30–33 cm)

Weight: 13–18 pounds (5.9–8.2 kg)

Coat and color: A long, silky coat with slight waviness is allowed. Four color varieties are recognized: solid red, red and white, black and tan, and tricolor.

The Cavalier King Charles Spaniel is a gentle house pet.

Grooming: The long coat needs brushing every few days. The large eyes sometimes need daily cleaning.

Temperament: This is a fearless, lively, athletic, and cheerful breed that is also fond of children. This spaniel is a very gentle and affectionate breed.

Exercise: Daily walks are necessary.

Chihuahua

The saucy Chihuahua is the world's smallest breed of dog. Native to Mexico, it was probably developed around the fifteenth century.

Appearance: Graceful, small, and compact, the Chihuahua has an alert terrierlike attitude.

Height: 6–9 inches (15–23 cm)

Weight: not to exceed 6 pounds (2.7 kg)

Coat and color: The short-haired variety has a glossy close-fitting coat. The long-coated variety has long, silky hair. Any color is acceptable.

Chihuahuas are the smallest dog breed in the world.

Grooming: Groom the smooth-coated Chihuahua's coat with a damp cloth. The silky hair of the long-coated Chihuahua needs to be brushed and bathed regularly.

Temperament: Very devoted to its owner, the lively Chihuahua is reserved with strangers. Some are bold; others are timid. They are sensitive to cold and seek out heat.

Exercise: The Chihuahua can get enough exercise running around indoors, but enjoys short walks and accompanying its owner on errands.

Chinese Crested Dog

Chinese Crested Dogs are uncommon and a most unusual breed of dog. The history of this breed's origin goes back to China some time in the twelfth century. Hairless dogs appear by mutation throughout the world but have principally been cultivated in Latin America and China. They were bred as rodent killers and lapdogs.

Appearance: A lively graceful dog with a narrow muzzle, the Chinese Crested is fine boned. There are two varieties. The Chinese Crested hairless has smooth, soft skin, which is pleasantly warm to the touch. The skin ranges from pink to dark brown and may also be spotted. The silky hair on its head may resemble a horse's mane or stand upright and is the source of the breed's crested name. The soft hair on its tail resembles a plume while that on the feet resembles socks. The Chinese Crested powder puff is the second variety. It has a full coat of hair.

Height: 11–13 inches (27–33 cm)

Weight: 5–12 pounds (2.3–5.4 kg)

Coat and color: Any color is allowed.

Grooming: The powder puff variety should be brushed every few days. The hairless dog needs regular skin care including moisturizer, sun block, and bathing to prevent blackheads.

Temperament: Sensitive and gentle, the breed has a boundless need for affection. Its paws, which resemble rabbits' feet, can tenderly embrace you. It is devoted to its owner but some are timid with strangers. These playful little dogs are also good with other dogs and pets. The hairless dogs are hearty eaters, as they need plenty of energy for increased production of heat. They are ideal pets for people who are allergic to dog hair.

Exercise: They need daily exercise and enjoy outdoor walks. The hairless variety is miserable in the cold and needs a warm sweater. A true sun lover, the hairless dog loves to bake in the blaz-

Chinese Cresteds are unique looking dogs. The Chinese Crested powder puff is the same breed with hair.

ing sun, which increases its risk of sunburn. The sun can sometimes turn the skin almost black.

Dachshund

The Dachshund is affectionately known as the "wiener dog." It was developed in Germany around the 1500s from a long-legged breed of hounds called Braques. Originally it was used to flush badgers, hence its European nickname of badger crawler. The long, low-slung body enabled the Dachshund to enter and easily move around inside a badger's burrow. Today it is primarily a family pet.

Miniature Dachshunds have very short legs.

Appearance: An elongated but sturdy dog with strong muscles and short legs. Despite its short legs, the Dachshund must have a fluid, smooth gait. There are two varieties: the standard and the miniature.

Standard Dachshund
Height: 8–9 inches (20–23 cm)
Weight: over 11 pounds (5 kg), usually 16–32 pounds (7.25–14.5 kg)
Miniature Dachshund
Height: 5–6 inches (13–15 cm)
Weight: 11 pounds (5 kg) and under
Coat and color: The short-haired or smooth Dachshund has a thick, close-fitting coat of hair. The wire-haired Dachshund has rough hair with a thick undercoat. The long-haired Dachshund must have a silky, soft coat of long hair, with long hair hanging from the backs of the legs and from the tail. For short- and long-haired Dachshunds, the most common colors are red (tan) and black with red markings. The wire-haired dogs come in all shades of brindle.

Grooming: The smooth Dachshund requires only occasional brushing. The wire-haired Dachshund's coat needs to be trimmed from time to time. To prevent the long-haired Dachshund's silky hair from becoming matted, daily brushing is necessary.

Temperament: Dachshunds are independent but enjoy their family's company. Many tend to be reserved with strangers. Bold and curious, they retain their interest in digging and hunting. This intelligent and adaptable breed responds best to positive training.

Exercise: Daily walks of moderate length are necessary. Its need for activity, especially while young, is great. The Dachshund greatly enjoys safe off-leash playtime outdoors.

French Bulldog

The toy English Bulldog is one ancestor of this breed developed as a companion in the 1800s. The toys fell out of favor with the English, but large numbers were sent to France where they were crossed with other breeds. The French Bulldog was the result, and the breed became very popular, particularly with women.

The French Bulldog is compact and muscular.

Its coat of hair is the trademark of the Havanese.

Appearance: The French Bulldog looks muscular and compactly built. The bat ear and flat skull between the ears are distinctive features of this earnest-looking breed. The tail is carried low between the legs.

Height: 11–13 inches (28–33 cm)

Weight: not to exceed 28 pounds (12.7 kg)

Coat and color: The coat is moderately fine, brilliant, short, and smooth. It is found in several colors including brindle, fawn, white, and brindle and white. Colors that include black are typically disallowed.

Grooming: A rubber brush can be used to remove dead hair, but the breed does not require much brushing.

Temperament: This breed likes to be part of family life. Well-mannered children and French Bulldogs can provide mutual companionship. They vary in their friendliness toward strangers—some are aloof while others are enthusiastically welcoming. Most are easy to train because they are willing to please. Other household pets are fine as long as the Bulldog

was socialized with them while young. Although they are not noisy and do not bark much, they are good watchdogs.

Exercise: Daily walks and indoor playtime are necessary. Because of their short muzzles, vigorous exercise in hot weather should be avoided.

Havanese

This dog belongs to the Bichon goup. The first Bichons probably came from the Mediterranean area to the Caribbean on merchant vessels. They continued to be bred on the island of Cuba. Over the centuries, they developed into a separate breed, the Havanese, or Bichon Havanais. After the Cuban revolution in 1959, many of these dogs were taken to the United States by people who left Cuba.

Appearance: The Havanese is a sturdy dog with short legs. The tail is covered in long soft hair and is carried over the back. The unique gait is characterized as springy and conveys the dog's happy nature.

Height: 8.5–11.5 inches (21–28 cm)

Weight: 7–13 pounds (3.2–5.9 kg)

Coat and color: The Havanese has a double coat. The soft coat of hair is loose and fluffy. The strands can range from straight to curly. The outer coat hairs can reach 6–8 inches (15–20 cm) in length. All colors and combinations are allowed.

Grooming: The hair has to be regularly brushed several times a week. If the hair is brushed against the coat to remove loose hairs, the hair will fall back into the desired position when the Havanese shakes itself after being brushed.

Temperament: The curious Havanese is always cheerful and in a good mood. Aggressiveness toward people and other dogs is rare. It is friendly and willing to please, which makes it a pleasure to train. This dog is very sensitive to mistreatment

Exercise: A moderate daily walk or an indoor play session provides sufficient exercise.

Italian Greyhound

Two thousand years ago, small Greyhounds were already common in Greece. The breed reached Italy in the Middle Ages. The Italian Greyhound was a favorite in the royal houses of Europe. Frederick the Great, King of Prussia, had as many as 40 Greyhounds.

Appearance: The Italian Greyhound is slender and elegant in appearance. The large expressive eyes cast a gentle look. This streamlined little dog is cold-sensitive because it has almost no fat insulation and a very thin coat. This small, long-limbed dog looks delicate.

Height: 13–15 inches (33–38 cm)

Weight: 7–14 pounds (3.2–6.35 kg)

Coat and color: The coat is short, glossy, and feels like satin to the touch. Except for brindle and black and tan, all colors and markings are acceptable.

Grooming: These dogs need little brushing except when shedding.

Temperament: The Italian Greyhound is high-spirited, alert, and courageous. In unfamiliar surroundings and with strangers, it is very reserved and cautious. This gentle and sensitive dog is good with well-mannered children. Gentle, consistent training is rewarded with a receptive pupil. Until they are about 18 months old, their bones are fragile and they can break a leg easily during rough play or when jumping down from heights.

Exercise: It loves to run and chase and caution should be used when allowing it to exercise off leash. Choose safely enclosed spaces for such activities.

The Italian Greyhound looks delicate and fragile.

The cheerful Japanese Chin is devoted to its owner.

Japanese Chin

The origin of this ancient breed has not been determined. The first dogs of this kind are believed to have come to Japan from China hundreds of years ago. They were kept and bred at the Japanese Imperial court.

Appearance: The Japanese Chin is a small, well-balanced, and aristocratic toy dog with a distinctive Oriental expression. The plumed tail is carried over the back. The stylish Japanese Chin is lively in movement.

Height: 8–11 inches (20–27 cm)

Weight: 4–7 pounds (1.8–3.2 kg)

Coat and color: The abundant coat is soft and straight. The coat has a thick mane on the shoulders and chest and the tail has abundant hair that forms an attractive plume. Black and white, red and white, and black and tan and white are the accepted colors.

Grooming: The long, soft coat needs regular brushing and combing to keep its silky luster. The eyes need daily cleaning.

Temperament: Cheerful and easygoing, the Japanese Chin enjoys cuddling on a lap and frolicking in the house. It is sensitive and devoted to its owner whom it tends to follow around like a shadow. The bright friendly nature of this breed extends to other dogs and to strangers. This breed is less temperamental than most toys. It is willing to please and enjoys being taught tricks. The Chin is uncomfortable in humid weather and tends to wheeze and snore.

Exercise: The Japanese Chin needs a daily walk or indoor play sessions.

King Charles Spaniel

King Charles II of England doted on the breed during his reign in the seventeenth century, hence its name. They flushed small birds as well as serving as foot and lap warmers.

Appearance: The breed has a prominent domed head with a pushed-back nose and a docked tail. Although similar looking to the Cavalier King Charles Spaniel, the King Charles Spaniel has a shorter muzzle.

Height: 10–11 inches (25–28 cm)

Weight: 8–14 pounds (3.6–6 kg)

Coat and color: Recognized colors are solid red, or black and tan, or either of these colors on white.

Grooming: The long coat should be brushed several times a week. The eyes should be cleaned every few days.

Temperament: Quiet and calm with its family, this breed is an affectionate lapdog that makes an excellent family pet. The King Charles' gentle nature typically extends to other household pets, especially when the spaniel is socialized with them while young. Some individuals are reserved with strangers, but after introductions, are quite friendly. An

Compared to the Cavalier King Charles Spaniel, the King Charles Spaniel has a shorter muzzle.

alert dog, the King Charles barks to announce visitors. However, it is not typically an excessive barker. Because of its short muzzle, it does not fare well in heat.

Exercise: Moderate daily walks are sufficient.

Lhasa Apso

This ancient breed originated in Tibet. Lhasa Apsos were bred in the monasteries as well as in the palace of the Dalai Lama. They performed several roles in the monasteries, including watchdog and companion. After World War I, some of these dogs came to England and the United States.

Appearance: The Lhasa's body is longer than tall and the tail is carried over the back. The dark intelligent eyes are hidden under a long fall of hair that can be pulled up in a topknot.

Height: 10–11 inches (25–28 cm), females slightly smaller

Weight: 13–15 pounds (5.9–6.8 kg)

Coat and color: The double coat consists of a fine undercoat and a heavier ground-length outer coat, which should be neither woolly nor silky. All colors are acceptable. The color of a puppy often changes as it grows older.

Grooming: Daily brushing and combing is essential. Professional grooming every few months is usually necessary. The hair above the eyes must be pulled up with a tie so it remains out of the eyes. Care must be taken that the ponytail is not pulled too tight or it will irritate the dog's skin. The eyes must be cleaned regularly. Unless its beard is kept trimmed, food remnants must be removed from its beard after eating.

Temperament: Affectionate and cheerful with its family, the Lhasa is proud, cautious, and reserved with strangers. Gentle and devoted, the Lhasa is content when sleeping beside its owner. It is an excellent watchdog with keen hearing, but without the reputation of excessive barking. The Lhasa is independent,

The Lhasa Apso is a frolicsome dog.

stubborn, and bold. It responds best to kindness and positive training to shape its good behavior. Some assertive individuals require a firm owner to counter their seeming willful disobedience.

Exercise: The lively Lhasa needs daily walks. However, the walks can be short and several play sessions of catch will often suffice.

Löwchen

The Löwchen is known as the "little lion dog." The exact time and origin of the breed are unknown. It is believed to have originated in France and Germany in the sixteenth century. Dogs resembling the Löwchen are often shown in sixteenth-century paintings. Löwchens were the companion of aristocratic ladies and gentlemen as well as bishops, then the breed fell into complete obscurity. A Belgian breeder reestablished breeding after World War II.

The typical appearance of the Löwchen, or little lion dog, requires professional grooming.

Appearance: The Löwchen received its nickname of "little lion dog" because ladies of the court groomed it to resemble a little lion. The Löwchen has a proud lively gait that accentuates the lion cut with a long, flowing mane.

Height: 12–14 inches (30–35.6 cm)
Weight: 8–18 pounds (3.6–8 kg)
Coat and color: The coat of hair is fairly long and wavy, but never curly. All colors and combinations are acceptable. White, black, gray, and lemon yellow are most common.

Grooming: The Löwchen needs brushing several times a week. Tangles should be gently combed out. Professional grooming is required several times a year. To maintain the traditional lion cut, professional grooming is required more often.

Temperament: This high-spirited, intelligent, and extremely affectionate breed is willing to please and devoted to its family. Some individuals are reserved with strangers. It responds well to consistent training.

Exercise: Short walks and indoor games are sufficient for the Löwchen. It enjoys playing off leash outside.

Maltese

From antiquity to modern times, the Maltese was the companion of elegant, fashionable ladies. Even today it is more of an indoor pet than a dog to take on extended walks.

Appearance: Covered from head to foot with a mantle of long white hair, the Maltese moves with a jaunty, smooth-flowing gait.

Height: 9–10 inches (23–25 cm)
Weight: under 7 pounds (3.2 kg), preferably 4–6 pounds (1.8–2.7 kg)

Coat and color: The pure white hair is silky and smooth. The hair hangs long and flat and

The Maltese's beautiful white coat requires time-consuming care.

larger dogs. Owners must protect their Maltese from such tendencies. It has a high watchdog quotient and some are excessive barkers. The Maltese is intelligent and fairly easy to train.

Exercise: The Maltese does not require vigorous exercise or long walks. Indoor games or short walks on a leash are sufficient.

Toy Manchester Terrier

This breed, also known as the Black and Tan Terrier, originated in the late 1800s in industrial regions of northern England. It was used to hunt small animals.

Appearance: This is a smooth-coated, elegant dog. It has a long, slender tail.

Height: 10–12 inches (25–30 cm)

Weight: under 12 pounds (5 kg), usually 6–8 pounds (2.7–3.6 kg)

Coat and color: The short, smooth coat of hair has a black ground color with mahogany-colored markings on the head, chest, and legs.

almost touches the ground. The dark eyes and nose contribute to its angelic expression. The hair above the eyes must be pulled up with a tie so it remains out of the eyes. Care must be taken that the ponytail is not pulled too tight or it will irritate the dog's skin. The hairs on its feet should be trimmed. To keep the coat tidy, gentle daily brushing is necessary. Tangles must be promptly removed to prevent matting. The eyes must be cleaned daily to prevent tears from discoloring the hair. Any leftover food caught in the beard must be removed after each meal.

Temperament: The consummate lapdog, the Maltese is gentle and affectionate. The Maltese loves to be in motion and is fond of running and playing, but it is more of an indoor pet than a dog that needs extended walks. While friendly and trusting with its family, the Maltese is reserved with strangers. The breed is typically fond of well-behaved, respectful children. The even-tempered Maltese is not high-strung nor is it timid. It can be bold and fearless for its size and sometimes challenges

The Toy Manchester Terrier was originally used to hunt small animals.

Grooming: Occasional brushing to remove dead hairs is sufficient.

Temperament: It is high spirited, vigilant, and friendly with children. When it encounters strangers, it is mistrustful but never aggressive. The Manchester Terrier needs consistency in training. This is a gentle and sensitive breed. It does not fare well in cold weather and appreciates a sweater and warm indoor bed.

Exercise: Daily walks on a leash are required.

Miniature Pinscher

The Miniature Pinscher belongs to the family of Pinschers and Schnauzers. It looks similar to the Doberman, but on a much smaller scale. Developed in Germany in the 1600s, the Miniature Pinscher hunted small rodents.

Appearance: This little dog is balanced, muscular, smooth, and clean lined. Its dark almond eyes are alert, soft, and intelligent.

The ears may be cropped or uncropped.

Height: 10–12.5 inches (25–31 cm), 11–11.5 inches (28–29 cm) preferred

Weight: 8–10 pounds (3.6–4.5 kg)

The Miniature Pinscher looks like a very small Doberman Pinscher.

Coat and color: The short smooth coat is lustrous. The color can be red, red with black hairs, and black with red markings.

Grooming: The coat requires minimal care, with only an occasional brushing to remove dead hair.

Temperament: This lively, intelligent breed is proud and self-possessed. Loyal to its primary caretaker, it is reserved with strangers. With a stubborn, independent nature, some individuals can be headstrong and require patience to train. The playful "Minpin" is not a lapdog and does not need to be pampered. However, it is sensitive to the cold and appreciates a sweater in cold weather. This vigilant little dog is quick to bark. Unless socialized with people while young, it tends to be suspicious of strangers.

Exercise: The Miniature Pinscher needs daily walks or several indoor play sessions.

Miniature Schnauzer

The Miniature Schnauzer was developed in Germany in the 1800s. At the end of the nineteenth century, it was exhibited for the first time at a dog show in Frankfurt, Germany. The better-known Affenpinscher was crossed with the Standard Schnauzer to develop this breed. Its original function was ratting.

Appearance: The Schnauzer has a rectangular head with a dark nose perched on the end of its muzzle. The ears are either cropped or small, folding, and V-shaped. Its eyes have black eyelid margins. The tail is docked.

Height: 12–14 inches (30–35.5 cm)

Weight: 13–15 pounds (5.9–6.8 kg)

Coat and color: The wire coat comes in three colors: salt and pepper, black and silver, or black.

Grooming: The coat needs to be plucked twice a year. Excessive hair between the pads of

The Miniature Schnauzer approaches even large dogs without fear.

the feet can be clipped. The longer hair should be combed to prevent tangles. The hairs around the mouth might need to be cleaned after each meal. Professional grooming is recommended. The hair in the ears should be removed.

Temperament: The playful and inquisitive Miniature Schnauzer is a popular breed. Lively, attentive, and intelligent, the Miniature Schnauzer can also be stubborn and willful, with its own ideas about following commands. Training should not involve repetitive drills. A confident owner who is fair and consistent does well with this breed. It is a well-mannered house dog that likes to be part of a family's activities. Vigilant and watchful, it has a loud bark; some may bark a lot. Most enjoy children. Although it can be socialized to other housepets, it can't resist the urge to chase a fleeing cat.

Exercise: The energetic Schnauzer needs moderate walks on leash or several game-playing sessions in the yard. It enjoys walks out of doors and spending time off leash in safe areas.

Papillon

This French breed originated as a lapdog in the 1500s. The French name *Papillon* means butterfly and refers to the face and ears of this toy dog. Two varieties occur. The type with erect ears is called the Papillon while the kind with drop ears is called the Phalene. Both types are acceptable, but the erect-eared dog is most popular. The early dogs had drop ears, but the erect ears gradually appeared. Except for their ears, the two types are identical in appearance.

Appearance: The fine-boned structure gives the Papillon its jaunty, dainty appearance. The long tail is carried arched over the body and is covered with a long plume.

Height: 8–11 inches (20–28 cm)

Weight: 9–10 pounds (4.1–4.5 kg)

Coat and color: The profuse coat of fine hair has a slight wave. There should be no undercoat. The hair is long and abundant on the ears, tail, and backs of the legs. The head is covered with short, smooth hair. The Papillon is always parti-color or white with patches of any color.

Papillons are very self-assured dogs.

Grooming: The Papillon's coat needs brushing several times a week. The eyes and ears should also be cleaned at regular intervals.

Temperament: The vivacious Papillon is very easy to train and is a popular obedience competition dog. It is charming and affectionate and friendly toward children, strangers, other dogs, and housepets. It adapts very readily to its family and enjoys human contact.

Exercise: Papillons love exercise and even extended walks and hikes are not a problem if the dogs are first properly conditioned.

Parson Jack Russell Terrier

This breed originated in England in the 1800s and was used for fox hunting both above and below ground. The terrier was named for Reverend John Russell, whose terriers trailed hounds. When the foxes went underground, the terriers bolted them back out so the hunt could continue.

Appearance: This delightful breed presents the picture of a self-assured, playful dog. The

The Parson Jack Russell Terrier is a playful and active breed.

docked tail is set high and its almond-shaped eyes glisten mischievously.

Height: 12–14 inches (30–35.5 cm)

Weight: 13–17 pounds (5.9–7.7 kg)

Coat and color: The Parson Jack Russell is double coated. Its coat can be either smooth or broken. Both types have a short, dense undercoat. The smooth variety has a flat, hard outercoat. The broken variety's outercoat is harsh, straight, tight, and close-lying. The color is white with tan, black, or brown markings.

Grooming: The coat is easy to care for and requires brushing only when the dog is shedding. The coat of the broken variety must be stripped occasionally to remove dead hairs.

Temperament: This active, intelligent dog is vigilant and bold. Its vociferous barking will announce the arrival of any strangers. It is quite self-confident and independent. Brave to the point of foolhardy, the dog must sometimes be protected from its tendency to find trouble. With its charming mischievous nature, this breed has increased in popularity. Although it can learn quickly, it is also independent minded. When training the Jack Russell, positive consistent training is necessary. Its hunting nature is still close to the surface and although it will coexist with household cats, its desire to chase can be provoked if the cat runs away.

Exercise: This breed needs more than simple walks on a leash around the block. It should be provided with a safely enclosed space for off-leash play as it will run off in search of adventure.

Pekingese

Only the Imperial family in ancient China had the right to keep these little lion dogs. These tiny dogs were often treated as royalty and were

Pekingese are confident dogs that can sometimes be stubborn.

pampered, with their own servants. Because they could be carried in the large sleeves of their Chinese owners' clothes, Pekingese were nicknamed "sleeve dogs." They were first brought to England in 1860, following the looting of the Imperial Palace by the British. One of the original lapdogs, the Pekingese still performs the same function as a companion.

Appearance: This compact little dog presents a lionlike image. The breed standard requires that the Pekingese convey its Chinese origin with directness, independence, and expression.

Height: 6–9 inches (15–23 cm)

Weight: not to exceed 14 pounds (6.35 kg)

Coat and color: The Pekingese has a thick undercoat with a long, coarse, straight outer coat. The outer coat forms a mane around the shoulders. All colors and patterns are allowed.

Grooming: To prevent mats, the coat must be brushed several times a week. The wrinkle above the nose should be cleaned each day. The hair around the anus should be checked daily for any soiling.

Temperament: Very self-assured and strong-willed, the dignified Pekingese can be difficult to train because of its deserved reputation for stubbornness. It is not a typical family dog. Although devoted, it is not necessarily affectionate.

Exercise: Short walks or indoor games are sufficient for the Pekingese. Because of the short nose, the Pekingese has difficulty breathing in hot or humid weather. It should be exercised indoors during such weather.

Pomeranian

The Pomeranian is a member of the Spitz group and might have descended from the sled dogs of Iceland and Lapland. It was developed as a companion in Germany in the 1800s.

Appearance: At first glance, you might think you see a small, round ball of hair on four legs approaching you. In reality, in the tiny body there still remains a fair amount of the cheeky

The Pomeranian's coat is easy to take care of, although it looks high maintenance.

German Spitz that today continues to live up to its reputation as an inexhaustible and undemanding guardian of houses and apartments. The tail is carried over the back and is covered with long hair.

Height: 8–11 inches (20–28 cm)

Weight: 3–7 pounds (1.4–3.2 kg), preferably 4–5 pounds (1.8–2.3 kg)

Coat and color: The Pomeranian's undercoat is cottony, soft, and dense. Its outer coat is long, straight, glistening, and harsh in texture. The coat is abundant over the shoulders and chest. The hair on the head and legs is shorter than that on the body. All colors and patterns are allowed.

Grooming: Its double coat needs brushing several times a week, more often when shedding.

Temperament: Pomeranians are attentive, lively, jaunty, and very affectionate with their owners, but they are mistrustful of strangers. They are quick to learn and easy to train. Good watchdogs, some also bark a lot.

Exercise: The Pomeranian is active, but its daily exercise needs can be met with indoor play or short walks.

Poodles are high-spirited, happy dogs.

Toy Poodle

Dogs resembling Poodles were known even in antiquity. Originating in central Europe, Poodles have been depicted in paintings since the sixteenth century. Around 1900 the first Poodle breeders' associations were established in Germany. After World War II the Poodle became popular in Europe and America.

Appearance: The outward appearance depends largely on the grooming cut. In the show ring, Poodles over 12 months are shown in either the continental or sporting clip.

Height: not to exceed 10 inches (25 cm)

Weight: 4–8 pounds (1.8–3.6 kg)

Coat and color: The Poodle's coat is curly with a naturally harsh texture. Any solid color is permitted.

Grooming: The Poodle needs to be brushed every few days. Professional grooming is recommended at least four times a year. The face and feet need to be trimmed once a month.

Temperament: The Poodle is very high-spirited, adaptable, and easy to train. Playful and intelligent, the Poodle is eager to please. It is sensitive and needs a lot of attention from its family. It is an outstanding watchdog, but never becomes aggressive.

Exercise: The Poodle needs daily exercise, which can be a walk on a leash, or several indoor games.

Pug

This ancient breed originated in China. Merchant ships brought the first Pugs to Holland around 1400; they then spread throughout Europe.

Appearance: The distinctive-looking Pug has a stocky body with deep wrinkles on the face and forehead. It has a short muzzle with a

The affectionate Pug has characteristic facial wrinkles.

The Schipperke is a watchful dog.

black mask. The tail is tightly curled over the hip.

Height: 10–11 inches (25–28 cm)

Weight: 14–18 pounds (6.35–8 kg)

Coat and color: The short coat is fine, smooth, and glossy. The Pug appears in three colors: silver, apricot-fawn, or black.

Grooming: The coat needs occasional brushing. The facial wrinkles must be cleaned daily.

Temperament: The friendly Pug is very affectionate and desirous of human contact. It is playful and confident. Sometimes comical, it can also be stubborn and headstrong. A Pug enjoys attention. It can be uncomfortable in hot humid weather. Because of its short muzzle, it wheezes and snores. Its prominent eyes can be accidentally injured in rough play.

Exercise: The pug needs consistent daily walks or several play sessions indoors.

Schipperke

The Schipperke was developed in Belgium around the 1600s as a vermin hunter and watchdog on barges and farms. This breed was mentioned in writings during the Middle Ages and is depicted in many paintings.

Appearance: The Schipperke is a small, thick-set dog without a tail. It has a foxlike face.

Height: male 11–13 inches (28–33 cm); female 10–12 inches (25–30 cm)

Weight: 12–16 pounds (5.4–7.25 kg)

Coat and color: A soft underlayer is present beneath a tough coat. It has a distinctive coat with a conspicuous ruff, cap, and culottes, which create the characteristic silhouette. The only color is black.

Grooming: The double coat should be brushed once a week. More frequent brushings are required when the dog sheds.

Temperament: The self-confident, bold Schipperke is curious and alert to what is going on in its environment. A loyal and devoted family dog, it is wary of strangers. A good watchdog, the Schipperke barks sharply at signs of trouble. Some can be excessive barkers and must be taught to stop barking. Some defend their territory against other dogs but are typically friendly with most dogs. Schipperkes accept cats and are usually good with children. Because they can be independent and headstrong, some are hard to train, but others are eager to learn.

Exercise: The lively Schipperke needs daily exercise and mental stimulation.

Scottish Terrier

The Scottish Terrier originated in Scotland in the 1800s and was developed to hunt vermin. In the late nineteenth century the first Scottish Terriers were exhibited at English dog shows. Soon thereafter, these dogs were also bred in the rest of Europe.

Appearance: The compact Scottish Terrier has a distinctive long head with erect ears, bushy eyebrows, and short beard. The dog seems to pack a lot of power in a small package.

Height: about 10 inches (25 cm)

Scottish Terriers need consistent, firm training.

Weight: male 19–22 pounds (8.6–10 kg); female 18–21 pounds (8–9.5 kg)

Coat and color: The Scottish Terrier has a double coat. The undercoat is soft and short. The topcoat consists of hard wiry hairs. Colors include black, wheaten, or brindle of any color.

Grooming: Its wire coat should be brushed several times a week. Professional grooming several times a year is recommended.

Temperament: Attentive and bright, sensitive and full of spirit, the Scotty is devoted to its family. It is vigilant, and some are mistrustful of strangers. Consistent training is essential. A typical fearless, feisty terrier, the Scottish Terrier can be aggressive toward other animals and enjoys digging.

Exercise: Daily walks or several rounds of indoor games are required. The Scotty enjoys outdoor exercise off leash in a safe, enclosed space.

Shih Tzu

This breed of lapdogs has ancient roots in China. Many legends are centered around the breeding of these temple dogs in Asia over the course of several millennia. The current Shih Tzu was developed in the 1800s during the reign of the Dowager Empress Cixi, whose name is pronounced Shih Tzu.

Appearance: The long, flowing coat of the Shih Tzu and its effortless movement contribute to an enchanting sight. The tail is carried over the back.

Height: 8–11 inches (20–28 cm)

Weight: 9–16 pounds (4.1–7.25 kg)

Coat and color: The Shih Tzu has a luxurious, dense double coat with long, flowing hair. A slight wave is permissible. Any color is acceptable.

The Shih Tzu's long hair should be tied on the top of its head.

Grooming: The Shih Tzu is high-mainte-nance and its long coat needs brushing every day. The hair above the eyes must be pulled up with a tie so it remains out of the eyes. Care must be taken that the ponytail is not pulled too tight or it will irritate the dog's skin. The eyes must be cleaned regularly. Unless its beard is kept trimmed, food remnants must be removed from its beard after eating. It is important that puppies be taught to accept, and ideally enjoy, grooming from a young age.

Temperament: Intelligent, lovable, and affectionate, the Shih Tzu is a sociable dog that enjoys its family. It can be somewhat independent and obstinate. Patience and con-sistency are necessary during training. Individ-uals vary in their friendliness toward strangers, probably in relation to their early socialization. The Shih Tzu is not typically a barker.

Exercise: Although small, the sturdy Shih Tzu still needs daily exercise. Short daily walks on a leash or indoor games with its owner are necessary. The short muzzle can cause difficulty breathing during hot humid weather.

Silky Terrier

This dog's Yorkshire Terrier ancestors were taken to the Australian states of Victoria and New South Wales in the late 1800s by English immigrants. The little terriers were used to hunt mice and other small animals. Crosses with indigenous Australian Terriers eventually resulted in the Silky Terrier.

Appearance: This Terrier's coat is striking and almost iridescent. The Silky is distinguish-able from the Yorkshire Terrier by its larger ears, more prominent muzzle, and longer back. In addition, it carries its tail higher and has hair of a slightly different color and length.

Height: 9–10 inches (23–25 cm)

Weight: 8–11 pounds (3.6–5 kg)

The Silky Terrier is often confused with the Yorkie.

Coat and color: The dog's coat is silky, long, smooth, and shiny. It has no underlayer. The accepted color is blue and tan. Silky Terriers are born black.

Grooming: The coat requires daily brushing and combing to maintain its good condition; expect to spend almost 15 minutes a day. The Silky does not shed much.

Temperament: Loyal and protective, the Silky Terrier likes to stay close to its primary caretaker. These dogs can be affectionate with their family and well-mannered children. They can be a pleasure to train as they are quick learners. This breed tends to bark a lot. Unless socialized with other household pets while young, some Silkies will not get along with other pets such as cats. Since they were bred to hunt, be cautious with pets such as rodents and rabbits.

Exercise: This is an active breed that requires daily walks on a leash or indoor games and attention.

Tibetan Spaniel

These little "lion dogs" lived in Tibetan monasteries. They turned the prayer wheels or sat guard on the monastery walls and reported anything out of the ordinary. This ancient breed first came to England at the end of the nineteenth century.

Appearance: The Tibetan Spaniel shares ancestors with the Pekingese. Its head, which is small in proportion to its body, is carried proudly. The feathered tail is set high on the body and carried over the back. It has expressive oval eyes.

Height: about 10 inches (25 cm)
Weight: 9–15 pounds (4.1–6.8 kg)
Coat and color: The Tibetan Spaniel has a double, long, silky coat. All colors and mixtures are acceptable, but golden is the most common color.

Grooming: A gentle brushing several times a week will keep the coat in good condition. The ears and eyes must be kept clean.

Temperament: Like all other Asiatic dogs, the self-assured Tibetan Spaniel has an unusual, almost fastidious catlike personality. It is good-natured and affectionate with its family. The sensitive Spaniel is intelligent and relatively easily trained. Consistency is important because it can sometimes be obstinate. These dogs get along well with children and other dogs. If socialized with cats while young, they can easily share a home. The vigilant Spaniel is an excellent watchdog. It is reserved and aloof with strangers.

Exercise: This breed does not need much exercise and indoor games or playtime in the yard will suffice. However, it enjoys short walks on a leash.

Exercise is important for the Tibetan Spaniel.

West Highland White Terrier

The "Westie" belongs to the group of Scottish terriers and was originally used for hunting predators. A Landseer painting dated 1839 is evidence that White Terriers were in existence as early as the beginning of the nineteenth century. In the painting, a Bloodhound and a White Terrier look out together from the inside of a doghouse. In the late 1800s, the Westie became well known as the partner of a Scottish Terrier in an advertising campaign for "Black & White" whiskey. It has since remained popular as a pet and showdog.

Appearance: A round head with small ears, dark eyes, and short muzzle in combination with a jaunty look in its eye characterizes the expression of this hardy terrier.

Height: male 11 inches (28 cm); female 10 inches (25 cm)

Weight: 15–21 pounds (6.8–9.5 kg)

Coat and color: The Westie has a double-layered coat. The undercoat is soft and short while the outercoat is rough and hard with no curls. This breed is always white with dark eyes and dark pigmentation on the pads of the feet, nails, and nose.

Grooming: The wire coat should be brushed a few times a week. Dead hairs need to be plucked from its coat two to three times a year. Professional trimming is recommended every three months. The Westie can be difficult to keep white if it spends time lounging on bare ground.

Temperament: The Westie is happy and curious, and enjoys being part of an active family. it is good with children because it can withstand some rough play. This is one of the friendliest terriers. Loyal to its primary caretaker, it is also friendly with strangers. The Westie is intelligent

The curious "Westie" is always white in color.

and relatively easy to train, but it has a tendency to be stubborn and independent. Firm, consistent training is important.

Exercise: The Westie needs plenty of outdoor exercise. It loves to chase a thrown ball and enjoys digging. Daily walks on a leash are necessary.

Yorkshire Terrier

The Yorkshire Terrier originated in England in the 1800s where it was developed to keep houses free of mice and rats. Its appealing appearance quickly made it popular with all levels of society.

Appearance: The Yorkie has hair that hangs down evenly and straight. The coat is parted from the bridge of the nose to the end of the tail. Its erect posture creates the impression of self-importance. The tail is docked to a medium length and carried slightly higher than the level of the back.

The Yorkie is a consistently popular breed.

Height: 8–9 inches (20–23 cm)

Weight: not to exceed 7 pounds (3.2 kg)

Coat and color: This breed has very long silky hair without an undercoat. The color is blue (steel gray) and tan (golden brown). As puppies, the gray hairs are black.

Grooming: The Yorkshire needs daily grooming of the coat with a brush. If the owner does not have enough time, the coat should be trimmed by a professional groomer. The hair above the eyes must be pulled up with a tie so it remains out of the eyes. Care must be taken that the ponytail is not pulled too tight or it will irritate the dog's skin. The eyes must be cleaned regularly. Hairs in the ears must be plucked or trimmed.

Temperament: Lively, intelligent, and courageous, the Yorkie is very attached to its family. This vigilant breed is very alert and readily barks quite loudly when it senses danger. The Yorkie is an intelligent pupil as long as consistent and positive training methods are used. It can get along with well-mannered children who respect the dog enough to leave it alone when it wants peace and quiet. Some Yorkies can be dangerously foolish in their courage toward larger dogs. If socialized properly while young, Yorkies can get along with cats but caution should be applied with small pets such as rodents and rabbits.

Exercise: Yorkies enjoy short walks on a leash, but many get enough exercise in their home, especially when their owner engages them in games.

INFORMATION

Organizations

To find the latest address, phone number, and web sites for the organizations listed, check the Internet.

American Kennel Club
5580 Centerview Drive
Suite 200
Raleigh, NC 27606
Phone (919) 233-9767
Fax: (919) 233-3740
E-mail: info@akc.org
Web site: *www.akc.org*

National Animal Poison Control Center
(888) 426-4435
($20.00 for five minutes and $2.95 per minute thereafter)

National Dog Registry
P.O. Box 118
Woodstock, NY 12498
(800) 637-3647

Home Again Microchip Registry (NDR)
(800) LONELY-ONE

Petfinders
368 High Street
Athol, NY 12810
(800) 223-4747

Books

American Kennel Club. *The Complete Dog Book.* New York: Howell Book House, 1997.

Arden, Darlene. *The Irrepressible Toy Dog.* New York: Howell Book House, 1998.

Baer, Ted. *Communicating with Your Dog*, 2nd ed. Hauppauge, NY: Barron's Educational Series, Inc., 1999.

Bailey, Gwen. *The Well-Behaved Dog.* Hauppauge, NY: Barron's Educational Series, Inc., 1998.

Coile, D. Caroline. *Encyclopedia of Dog Breeds.* Hauppauge, NY: Barron's Educational Series, Inc., 1998.

Rice, Dan. *Small Dog Breeds.* Hauppauge, NY: Barron's Educational Series, Inc., 2002.

Smith, Cheryl S., and Stephanie J. Tauton. *The Trick Is in the Training.* Hauppauge, NY: Barron's Educational Series, Inc., 1998.

UC Davis. School of Veterinary Medicine. *Book of Dogs: A Complete Medical Reference Guide for Dogs and Puppies.* New York: HarperCollins Publishers, Inc., 2002.

Wood, Deborah. *Little Dogs: Training your Pint-Sized Companion.* Neptune City, NJ: TFH, 2004.

Periodicals

Dog Fancy Magazine
P.O. Box 6050
Mission Viejo, CA 92690

Dog World
P.O. Box 6050
Mission Viejo, CA 92690

About the Authors

Armin Kriechbaumer, who has bred small dogs successfully for many years, is publisher of *Klein-hundewelt*, a specialty periodical. He serves as a specialty judge at dog shows.

Sue Fox is a wildlife biologist and a freelance writer. She is the author of more than 15 books on the care of pets, including hermit crabs, gerbils, and dogs. She shares her home with a variety of animals, including several hunting dogs.

Photo Credits

Norvia Behling: 13, 22, 24, 25, 33, 34, 39, 46, 56, 62, 73 (top), 84, 86, 87 (left), 89 (top), and 91; Tara Darling: 7 (top and bottom), 9, 11, 14, 17, 18, 19, 20, 21, 26, 27, 30, 37, 38, 40, 41, 42, 43, 47, 48 (left and right), 49, 51, 52 (left and right), 53, 60, 61, 63, 69, 81 (top), 85 (top and bottom), 87 (right), 89 (bottom), and 90; Cheryl Ertelt: 2–3, 4, 5, 6 (top and bottom), 36, 54, 57, 58, 59, 68, 70 (bottom), 71 (right), 73 (bottom), 74, 82, 83 (bottom), 88, and 92; Isabelle Francais: 8, 31, 55, 70 (top), 72, and 76 (left), 79 (top); Gorski: 77; Inter-topics: 78; Lanceau: 71 (left); Reinhard: 79 (bottom); Bob Schwartz: 73 (top); Thompson: 75 and 81 (bottom); and Wilbie: 76 (right), 80, and 83 (top).

Important Note

This pet owner's manual tells the reader how to buy or adopt, and care for small dogs. The authors and publisher consider it important to point out that the advice given in this book is meant primarily for normally developed dogs of excellent physical health and good character.

Anyone who adopts a fully grown dog should be aware that the animal has already formed its basic impressions of human beings. The new owner should watch the animal carefully, including its behavior toward humans, and should meet the previous owner.

Caution is further advised in the association of children with dogs, in meeting with other dogs, and in exercising the dog without proper safeguards. Even well-behaved and carefully supervised dogs sometimes do damage to someone else's property or cause accidents. It is therefore in the owner's interest to be adequately insured against such eventualities, and we strongly urge all dog owners to purchase a liability policy that covers their dog(s).

Cover Photos

Norvia Behling: inside front cover, inside back cover, and back cover; Isabelle Francais: front cover.

Second English-language edition published in 2005 by Barron's Educational Series, Inc. First English-language edition published in 1994 by Barron's Educational Series, Inc.

All inquiries should be addressed to:
Barron's Educational Series, Inc.
250 Wireless Boulevard
Hauppauge, NY 11788
www.barronseduc.com

International Standard Book No. 0-7641-3099-4

Library of Congress Catalog Card No. 2004062448

Library of Congress Cataloging-in-Publication Data
Kriechbaumer, Armin.
[Kleinhunde. English]
Small dogs : everything about history, purchase, care, nutrition, training, and behavior / Armin Kriechbaumer and Sue Fox ; full color photographs, illustrations by Renate Holzner.—2nd English language ed.
p. cm.
Includes bibliographical references.
ISBN 0-7641-3099-4 (alk. paper)
1. Toy dogs. I. Fox, Sue, 1962– II. Title.

SF429.T7K7513   2005
636.76—dc22   2004062448

Printed in China
9 8 7 6 5 4 3 2 1